The Spirit Baby
Diaries

By Katie Ubele

The Spirit Baby Diaries

info@katiewilliamsintuition.com
Katie the Creatress LLC

Disclaimer:
This book is intended to provide helpful and informative material on the subjects addressed. It is not a substitute for professional medical, psychological, or legal advice. The author, editor, and publisher are not responsible or liable for any actions or results taken by any person, organization, or entity on the basis of information contained in this book. All readers are advised to seek services of competent professionals in the appropriate field.

Library of Congress Number: 2024922917

ISBN: 979-8-218-52750-1

First Edition: December 2024

Cover design by Katie the Creatress LLC
Interior design by Katie the Creatress LLC

Printed in the United States of America

To the women who mother, will mother, women who love deeply, and the women with a fascination for our world and beyond

Love,

Katie Ubele

Note from the author:

Why do you want to be a parent? Or, what made you want to become a parent if you are one already? I know, it's a tough question to answer because it doesn't often feel like it could be reasoned with through a logical response. It just feels like a... calling.

I've often wondered what that calling feels like as it varies from person to person. I wonder if for them it felt like a whisper, or a "pinch me" moment, or if the desire didn't come until a pregnancy came unexpectedly.

My calling to become a mom was a classic, "I woke up and wanted to become a mom." Except, I was 13.

It was around this time too where I dove into the rabbit hole of spirituality and manifestation. (Thank you internet for throwing my teen mind for a loop. It worked out!) My own intuition was beginning to naturally develop. It started off innocent. I would dream about exact test scores I'd get in school, then receive it back the next day with the exact score I dreamed. However, I also like to believe that the sudden desire to become a mom was my intuition leading me down this path of becoming an author and spirit baby medium.

Fast forward to 2016.
"Kate!" my teacher announced. I sharply lifted up my

head, gathered my red composition notebook, and half-walk half-tiptoed my way over to my teacher's desk. I stood in front of her desk swaying as she read the essay scripted into my notebook. You see, when she gave us 15 year olds the prompt of writing about our biggest aspirations, the murmurs I heard around the room consisted of the words, "college," "independence," and "career." Meanwhile, my mind was saying, "Marriage. Motherhood. Children."

When her eyes scanned the final words on the page, her neck remained stiff and she raised only her eyes at me. "That's all you want to do?" she asked.

I replied with a shy, "yes," unable to gather any more words than I had already expressed on the page. Little did I know at the time that my dream to become a mother, would only expand and help other women fulfill their dream of motherhood.

Fast forward to when I was 18, I switched colleges 3 times in under a year. At the time I was pursuing a dance teaching career. I couldn't shake an undeniable feeling of a void as I walked into my 9am ballet class, or took an afternoon walk around campus feeling unable to relate my true desires deep down of being a wife and a mother to those around me. That year, at the beginning of 2020, the pandemic occurred. At this same time, an acquaintance of mine from dance shared a post by an intuitive reader. Even though I was familiar with spirituality and manifestation, the terms, "Intuitive" and "Energy Healing" were entirely new to me. I booked a reading, and from there I was hooked!

I began taking intuition training during the first half of 2020 and was submerged in feelings of fulfillment. For the first time, it didn't feel like I was suppressing what I truly desired, but that somehow what I was beginning to learn was supporting it.

Another woman I followed online at the time was sharing the journey of her first pregnancy, and that is where I heard the term "spirit baby." I learned that a spirit baby is the consciousness of our future child, and that we can connect with them before birth, or even conception!

A little whisper said, "Well what if... I can learn more about this, and THEN I can use my new intuitive tools to connect with my future children!!" *Cue triumphant Hallelujah music*

After beginning to learn about spirit babies, I purchased my first angel oracle card deck. Every night I had a ritual of applying what I was learning in my intuitive reader training to connecting with my spirit babies. Synchronicities began to occur. I'd ask my cards if my spirit babies were present. The "yes" card would fall out of the oracle deck. I'd ask the universe to show me a ladybug within 24 hours if my spirit babies were near. I'd see a ladybug. Patterns began to form as I allowed my curiosity to soar and explore!

The idea for this book came at that time.

As I became more confident in my gifts, I began doing readings for others. Up until that point, I had never felt the amount of joy in my heart as I did when emails like, "The name you mentioned in the reading is one I have loved!," came through, or when I witnessed the ear-to-ear smile on a client's face as she delightfully shared, "Katie, I'm pregnant!!"

At the time of this book's release, in late 2024, I am newly married and calling in my spirit babies.

No matter what stage of life you are in, spirit babies are always ready and excited to connect. All you have to do is reach out!

It doesn't matter if you are 16 years old wanting to become a mother one day, an intuitive reader calling in extra support into your sessions, or a mother conceiving her 4th child. Spirit babies operate at a level of high consciousness and awareness. Even though they may become a baby to us physically, their wisdom extends beyond lifetimes.

What you are about to read is a collection of channelings from one of the most fascinating realms:

The Spirit Baby realm. This realm is a place that is quite intangible to our human senses, yet a state of time and being where souls are choosing to step into a new identity and purpose in the form of becoming a human. Collectively, the spirit baby realm is on a mission in the 21st century to spiritually advance society and to raise the consciousness of the planet. This means helping humanity to raise their vibration. A vibration, emitted similar to sound waves, is a measurement of energy. The average person vibrates at around 200hz. Recent generations have been learning to raise their vibration to 400, which is matched with the energy of neutrality. The spirit babies who will be conceived from now to the next 2-3 generations will be coming in to move the vibration up to 500-600hz, which operates in the frequency of love.

The chapters you will be reading are a collective of conversations between the spirit baby realm and I. Spirit babies are highly open, honest, and excited to communicate with us. The conversations will include my description of the spirit babies as they present themselves to me through my psychic senses. I hope you feel the divine love they exude.

My intention for this book is to initiate conversations around what is beyond the 3D, and who we are outside of our physical bodies. I invite you to open your mind and take what resonates, and leave what does not. This book is not about what is right, or wrong, or truth, but a documentation inspired by the desire to *find* the truth of who we are.

I hope this book fills you with a plethora of wisdom to connect you to the child destined to be yours, or the ones in spirit guiding you every step of the way. Enjoy!

Terms to Know:

Chakra: A chakra is a point of energy within the body. In Sanskrit it means "wheel." Working with chakras have become part of modern day spirituality and yoga teachings. The teaching of chakras originated in India between 1500 and 500 BC in a text called the Vedas. There are 7 main chakras, each with a different color and function. There is also a correlation between each chakra, and a system within the body. (ex. reproductive system)

Root Chakra (Red, Symbolizes Being Grounded, Stability, and Foundations): Located at the base of the spine

Sacral Chakra (Orange, Creativity, Sexuality, Enjoyment) : Located in the lower abdomen

Solar Plexus Chakra (Yellow, Confidence, Regulation, Power) : Located below the ribs

Heart Chakra (Green, Love, Compassion, Empathy) : Located in the center of the chest

Throat Chakra (Light Blue, Expression, Communication, Openness) : Located at the base of the throat

Third Eye Chakra (Indigo, Intuition, Perception, Vision) : Located in between the eyebrows

Crown Chakra (Deep purple, Connection to Spirit, Knowledge, Thoughts) : Located just above the top of the head

Frequency: A frequency describes the pattern of waves (such as sound waves) over a period of time. Frequencies are measured in hertz (Hz.) Everything has a frequency from sound, to our emotions, and beyond.

Dimension: Quantum physics theorizes that our universe contains 11 dimensions. A dimension is a way of describing a space. Each of the 11 dimensions contain a different depth of the functionality of time, space, and gravity. We are three dimensional beings. This means we can move up, down, left, and right, but time continues in a "forward" direction and we cannot change or move.

4th dimensional beings and beyond can experience time like a direction.

Realm: A realm can harness the "rules" of any of the 11 dimensions. The difference is that a realm inhabits other beings. You can think of a dimension like open land, and a realm would be a house on the land. A realm is created through similar electrical charges coming together and creating its own container of energy. Imagine a larger magnet picking up many smaller ones that become joined together.

Yoni: Yoni is a Sanskrit word that translates to "womb." However, this word is also used to describe the vagina.

Contents

Part 3: Short Lessons and Transmissions

Part 4: Embodying Agape

Set an Intention

Before we begin

Setting an intention is the process of deciding to receive something we wish to manifest, heal, or gain clarity on.

It lets the universe, and our spirit babies, know where our heart currently lies and what outcome we would like to have.

Part 1:

Meeting the Unborn

Chapter 1: What is the spirit baby realm?

Me: "Hello Spirit Baby Realm! Which spirit baby would like to come forth today?"

Spirit Baby: "Hello! My name is Mikah. I was an architect in my previous lifetime in Italy. It is wonderful to meet you!"

Mikah presents himself in the identity of his past life as the architect. He presents his aura as round and full of pure white light. Physically, he presents the face of a healthy older man in his 50s. At the moment I type this, he is acknowledging to me that he still very much embodies his previous identity because he is proud of the life he led.

Me: "Thank you for joining us today! I am currently writing a book about the Spirit Baby Realm. You are the first spirit baby to come forward."

*Mikah smiles with delight, and his face is full of serenity

Me: "Could you explain what the Spirit Baby Realm is? I would love to give the readers a tangible understanding of where spirit babies come from!"

*Another spirit appears from behind Mikah on his right side. He introduces her as Colleen, his wife from his previous lifetime. He says that she loves hearing him lecture and educate! Colleen is the name she has chosen to be addressed by when communicating with her future parents.

Mikah: "When a soul approaches this realm who is still holding on to hurt from their past life, the rest of us feel heavy. That soul will not be welcome into the realm. We do not shame or judge that soul. We simply let them know that they are not ready. The space around us is gray and dull. It feels like breathing in heavy fog. But then, when all of us are working together, feeling happy, or are one step closer to coming to Earth, we are showered in golden light. Like a plane taking off, our aura feels uplifted in every way. When you go into meditation to access the spirit baby realm, you may see a castle or a similar structure. You must know that this castle isn't 'real.' It is your mind forming an image to represent what your soul knows and feels. The spirit baby realm is where we come when we are preparing for our next lifetime. You may see, I look and sound very much like myself from my previous life. This is because I quite enjoyed that life, and wanted to share it with you! Let me show you around this realm."

*Mikah gestures to "follow" him with my third eye

Mikah: "To your human self, what we have set up may seem like a factory, yet that couldn't be further from the truth. We have a place for choosing a personality, a place for choosing parents, a place for learning about current Earthly societies, and quite anything you can imagine! Each place is a formation of intention. When each of us intends to do one of these tasks, the options will appear. Imagine these options as feeling like different emotions or sensations in your body. This is how we interpret and choose these options. For example, one option may feel like a fluttering heart.

Another may feel like a sick, bloating belly. The fluttering heart would be the choice!"

Me: "Thank you Mikah for showing me around! You brought up some things I am going to dive into further in the book. I appreciate your guidance today."

Mikah: "Thank YOU my dear! Come again!"

Chapter 2: What is a Spirit Baby?
(Plus, an energy practice for you to use!)

I invite you to do this practice with me, so you can begin connecting to the spirit baby realm as well! Imagine 300 feet above your head an enormous ocean of golden light. See the golden light creating a funnel as it begins to pour into your head. Allow this golden light to flow into your entire body. Now, bring your attention to the very center of the Earth. See a bright, pastel pink ball of light. Visualize this ball of light sprouting up from the Earth, into the bottoms of your feet, then throughout your body.

Set the intention that all energy that is not serving you in this moment is being removed from your body and blowing up into sapphire blue and white light. Notice tiny fragments of indigo light piece themselves into the shape of a ball in front of your third eye. See this ball being penetrated by the golden and pink light we visualized earlier. Allow this ball of light to come into your third eye and into your mind. Feel a shower of white light cleanse your entire body. Then, put on your energetic shield! We are going to create a 4-layered energetic shield. This ensures that we are remaining in our own body, energy, and are able to have a distinction between ourselves and anything that we are channeling or connecting to.

See a golden ball of light come down in front of your body, stopping at the solar plexus.

Push this golden ball of light around your body. Next, do the same with a white ball of light. Now with a liquid mirror, seeing the mirror part facing away from you. Then the last layer of a sapphire blue flame. Finally, see the entire room or space that you are in being coated in a glittering, royal purple light.

The final step of seeing the purple light is one that I use specifically for connecting with spirit babies!

Now, we are going to set the intention to connect with the spirit baby realm.

Close your eyes, place your hand on your heart or your womb, and say out loud or in your mind, "I set the intention to connect to the spirit baby realm."

Repeat this statement until you feel you are connected. This may feel like a gut feeling, inner knowing, or a state of calm.

Each time you read the pages in this book, you may choose to do this practice if you want to channel from the spirit baby realm as you read what they have to say here. Let's connect with another spirit baby!

A soul comes forward with the shape of a female. She shares her name is Martha. Her appearance is tall, angelic (she has golden wings resembling that of a bird), and her face is not clear. Her frame is much larger compared to the other souls she is surrounded by.

As I type this outside, a bird has landed right in front of me.

Me: "Hi Martha! Thank you for joining us today!"

She places her palms together in a gesture of gratitude.

Me: "Could you explain what it means to be a spirit baby? It is a term that we use here to describe souls that are choosing to come into their next lifetime, however it would be lovely to hear it from your perspective."

Martha: "Your intention is lovely sweet one. Thank you for consulting with us, and with I, today. You may have noticed my peculiar appearance. I am a leader for the souls here. I transition them, like a doula in your world, to transverse the realms and join Earth. I see that you are curious about why I am angelic. You may not consider me a spirit baby because I am not planning on my next lifetime. However, my intention of helping other souls allows me to cross planes between the Spirit Baby Realm, and offering guidance on Earth. A spirit baby is a soul who is ready to face the next karmic life cycle. Do not fear the word karma. Karma is simply give or take, duality, and a mirror. In fact, the souls whom you consider a spirit baby are quite delighted to take on the task of enduring another lifetime. You may notice the words I am using here seem forceful, however in our world these words only have the meaning we intend for them to have. So the word "endure", to us, means to flow. It means to be present inside that of a physical body, and experience what that physical body can do.

A spirit baby is a soul who has made peace with their previous lifetime, no matter if they were considered to be a good or a bad person. Everyone is neutral here."

Me: "A previous guide said that some souls come with heavier energy and are not welcomed around spirit babies. Is that true, even though every soul is neutral?"

Martha: "Every soul you see here has a clean slate. While they are imprinted with the memories, triumphs, and feats of previous lifetimes, they are not attached to them. Nor are they attached to what their next lifetime will be. The souls you described are not spirit babies. They are crossed over souls. You may wonder as to how these souls were still able to access the spirit baby realm, yet not fully. We run off of a lot of intentional energy. And so, because those souls had the intention for a moment or two to become a spirit baby, they were able to feel the essence of this realm. However, that does not mean that they have fully separated from the identity of their previous lifetime.

To continue with sharing what a spirit baby is, imagine the air you breathe on Earth. It is invisible, yes? But you can still feel it, hear it, possibly even taste it. A spirit baby's energetic makeup is similar to air. Imagine if the air could choose where it would travel next. That is quite similar to the essence, and presence, of a spirit baby. So when you connect with us, you may feel a cool breeze, a tingling in the heart, or a release of tension.

In fact when you connect with a spirit baby, you are quite literally breathing them in. This is nothing to worry about or prevent. Spirit babies desire to be in a physical body on Earth, and this is their way of getting a glimpse, other than pregnancy, to be part of your realm. When a spirit baby does this, they are not taking over your being, body, or individuality. This is because their intentions are pure, and out of sheer curiosity. Just as effortlessly as you inhale their energy, you can exhale. You can decide where they dwell in your body as you are connecting to them. Or, if you prefer separation, you may let them know when initially making a connection."

Me: "Martha, you have been extremely helpful today. Your guidance is astounding! I will keep you in my thoughts as a soul who is greatly helping spirit babies come to Earth, especially with the excitement of the frequency raising on the planet!"

Martha: "You are very welcome. See you soon!"

Chapter 3: The Cycle of a Soul

I am extremely excited for us to channel this next question because, if your mind dives deep like mine, you might be wondering, "How is a soul created?" "What makes a soul conscious?" "What is the life cycle of a soul?" This chapter is going to be dedicated to answering those questions. Take a moment and do the energetic practice from the previous chapter. Then when you are ready, continue reading!

As I am connecting to the spirit baby realm, it seems they are very busy today. Every soul is zooming around and working in unison. It seems that they are rearranging, and I am hearing them say they are working on shifting frequencies. When they say this, they are referring to being prepared with enough wisdom and knowledge to keep their baseline vibration high after coming into the human body. This is because once here on Earth, not only do we have a soul but we also have a human brain that influences our reality, decisions, and experiences. These souls are ensuring that throughout their experiences on Earth, they will for sure come back to living in a higher frequency and spiritually healthy way of living. Let's request a spirit baby to come forward.

Take a few moments to set the intention with me.
A playful soul with the voice of a little girl approaches. She says "Hi!" in an excited voice.

Me: "Hi there! I am writing a book on the spirit baby realm and I would love it if you have the time to discuss how a soul is created, and the cycle a soul goes through along their journey!"

Soul: "Sure! My name is Fana. Oh boy... where do I begin? Okay, so let me explain where we come from in the first place. Like whooo are we? What the heck is a soul? So first let's look at the stars! Each star gives off a speck of electricity. When a few of these little specks come together, it starts to create a soul! A soul is a form of energy that is aware. So, just like how me and you are talking right now, we are aware of this. We know it's happening. For you as a human, you have little circuits of electricity running through you right now to your brain. Think of that, but without the human body. Just purely as energy! Once the soul is created, it begins to drift off. A lot of souls drift towards the moon. A soul will drift to whichever planet, star, or galaxy is matching the current wavelength that they are giving off. Because let's remember, souls don't just incarnate as human beings. There are millions of beings throughout multiple universes. Some universes are being created now as we speak, and many souls are excited for the beauty those universes are going to bring! Anyway, I digressed."

Me: "I'd love to pause you right there! How does a soul decide to come to Earth? And will a soul forever incarnate on Earth?"

Fana: "Oh heck no! We don't stay in one place!

A soul goes where it is called. It goes where there is a magnetism between the wavelengths like we discussed. Earth specifically has a very unique frequency. Only the bravest of souls go to Earth. It's super weird, you can imagine it like a challenging but rewarding video game. Many souls look upon Earth and are terrified of what it is like to be there. They are not scared because of what happens on Earth, but they can't fathom the amount of growth they will experience there. The souls who are gravitated to Earth give off a lot of pressure in their aura. In your world, it's like if you shake up a soda can but don't yet open the cap. It's just waiting and waiting to come out! Going to Earth is like that explosion. It releases the pressure and completely transforms the soul in a way that then benefits the other realms. From that point forward, there's a cycle of death and rebirth. This happens to all life forms that exist in a body. A body is like a blueprint of energy. And that energy can multiply and reproduce. After a death, the soul can then decide what they want to do from there. Some souls are ready for their next lifetime. Some souls need some time to stay in the identity of the previous life. Some souls decide to do spiritual work as guides or angels. We all choose something different, based on what our soul is pulled towards and what other planets, galaxies, and other places need. When you go through a death and rebirth, the rebirth is stronger every time. So each time you live a life and you pass on from that life, you have more knowledge and more wisdom. At times, the effect you had on those around you is active in your aura. That is one of the factors that affect how quickly a soul moves to their next lifetime, or if they have the capacity to carry out spiritual work.

Souls, including you, want to live more lives. When you live more lives, you have more to give. You also have more room to receive. It brings you closer to having more influence and power in the highest vibrational ways! That is it for today. I have much work today with the other souls. Thank you so much for dropping by and your presence is always welcomed!"

Me: "Before you go, I noticed that your voice and tone changed the more we spoke. When you first introduced yourself, you gave the impression of a young girl. The more we spoke, the more grown up you sounded. Why is that?"

Fana: "It's because the more I talked to you, the more I became attuned to your energy. My aura is very malleable right now as I am very close to coming to Earth, so I tend to take on some of the characteristics of those I speak to who are in a body."

Me: "That is very eye opening! Thank you for sharing, and good luck on your journey to Earth."

Fana appears as a rounded, blue shape floating like a balloon and she blows a kiss, then swiftly drifts away.

Chapter 4: Is there a heaven and a hell?

I feel called today to call in one of my own spirit babies to respond to this question. Since I'll be connecting with one of my spirit babies, names will be kept private. I have already connected with them and asked the question, so let's begin!

"I don't think humans understand how complex this question can be. Heaven and hell can practically exist wherever you want it to. It's up to you to decide. Here in the spiritual realms, we do have a place we can call heaven. But the reason why this is heaven is because spirit babies, spirit guides, and angels alike are sharing the same frequency. Heaven is the place we go to when we are feeling like we are on top of the world. It is an experience every soul desires to have. But you have it on Earth too! When you think positive thoughts, or explore something new that brings you joy, you are feeling into heaven. When you feel down, at your lowest point, you are feeling into hell. After a soul crosses over, many will be able to experience heaven. Some don't until after a few life cycles. By life cycles I mean experiencing the process of being born in a physical body, then dying, and repeating it over a few times. Each life cycle raises the frequency of a soul more and more. That is because the soul has more to give, more room to receive, and a more developed aura.
A soul experiences hell when they have difficulty crossing over. You might see it in those silly tv shows where there are ghost hunters and ghosts wandering around spaces that they can't seem to let go of.

This is because when a soul crosses over, they have a team of guides and angels to assist them. You could say that the souls who have trouble crossing over skipped a step before coming to Earth. As a soul, we are very malleable. We can take in just about any type of energy. We take on a lot of energies when we are exploring Earth, or any other physical plane, before coming into the human body. Some souls forget to maintain their own energetic baseline, and aren't open to attracting the guides and angels who will assist them when they leave their physical body.

A soul who is having difficulty crossing over, or in this sense we can say when they are in hell, it is important to have a loving team of people who can help them. This requires highly skilled people who understand how to work with souls. Not having the ability to ascend into a higher frequency and join heaven, the spirit baby realm, or becoming a spirit guide is hell. What we see today with people chasing down souls is actually creating more resistance and keeping them in hell. If a loving team of psychics get together and assist the soul in fully leaving the physical plane, the soul will no longer feel suffering and be able to continue their cycle. Heaven, on the other hand, is definitely a place that feels like a reward. It is not about how good or bad you are, but how evolved your aura is. Naturally, with time and experience, more wisdom is evolved. We are living in a wonderful time because many souls who have made it to heaven are choosing to come back to Earth in this century. Oftentimes, once a soul vibrates on the heavenly frequency, they will choose to stay there.

So what we are seeing today is something that is incredibly rare, but much needed for Earth; and that is what influences souls' decisions whether to stay in Heaven or not. If they feel something is needed, whether it be Earth or another planet or realm, they will go with no questions asked and no hesitance.

Heaven is a place where we celebrate. Again, these places are spaces that are created by a collectively aligned frequency. Many spiritual leaders you may know of exist in Heaven. They each have their own 'rooms' within Heaven. Think of Heaven like a huge house or mansion and each room is designed uniquely. Everyone gathers there, but each person may be drawn to a different room. When a soul gets to Heaven, there is no relaxing! This is where the real work begins! But this work is the most euphoric thing a soul could ever do. They repair energetic gaps around places like Earth to ensure peace has room to be created, help other souls prepare for their next lifetime, and guide others on the Earthly plane. Many souls from Heaven will offer protection from lower frequencies. When you call upon angels, those angels are souls that are highly advanced with thick skin, or shall I say aura, that can repel lower frequencies. They love what they do, and are always here to guide, serve, and protect."

Chapter 5: A soul's purpose

Contemplating the question, "What is my purpose?" is something that many of us can relate to! If you're someone who becomes fascinated and engulfed with multiple things, raise your hand! Personally, I've gone from wanting to become a dancer, to a teacher, to an ultrasound technician, back to a dancer, and repeating the process of trying to 'figure out' my purpose all over again. Tapping into the spirit baby realm taught me that the concept of having a purpose isn't as three dimensional as we approach it.

Let's get connected with the soul who will paint the picture for us on what it means to have a soul purpose, and how spirit babies choose theirs! Also remember that you were once a spirit baby, and you went through this process as well.

The spirit baby joining us today is different from the other souls we have communicated with! This soul presents himself as a young boy, and he speaks in colors. As he is greeting me, he is doing front flips in the air and giving off waves of rainbow colors. Since he is communicating in a way that isn't clairaudient (the psychic sense of hearing), I am tuning into my clairsentience (the psychic sense of touch) to translate his pictures and frequencies into words.

When I ask him to describe a soul's purpose, he fans out the rainbow colors so that each color has its own individual ray. Through this fan of rainbow colors, he is sharing that a purpose is multi dimensional.

It doesn't fit into a box. Another soul is approaching, and she shares that she was his mother in a previous lifetime. She will be joining him in his next lifetime, but this time as his sister!

"Hello!" she greets me, "I see you have found your way into my brother's frequency. He can be quite a handful, and he is trying out his wide range of expressions for when he comes to Earth. I believe it suits him quite well!"

Her tone of voice is one that is cheerful, bubbly, and nurturing.

"I know exactly what he is expressing," she continues, "but allow me to put into words the answer to your question."

She spins around and ascends higher up, lifting her posture as she shows a big smile on her face.

"A soul's purpose is ever changing when we look at the grand scheme of things. A soul will choose a different purpose with each lifetime, which is dependent on what Earth or another physical plane needs at that time. For example, my last purpose came in the form of being a mother. But being a mother wasn't my purpose. Being warm, nurturing, and healing other peoples' bodies was. I was a nurse before becoming a mother, but you could say I was a bit of a medicine woman! I was obsessed with herbal treatments to help patients. Being a nurse suited me in the chapter of life I was in, then once I had children, I fulfilled my purpose in a different way.

A purpose isn't about becoming something physical or putting yourself into a box. A purpose is about who you are. Both as a nurse and a mother, I was fulfilled. My greatest gifts had room to shine. And I don't regret any of it. I followed my heart. That is what everyone should do. If you look at my brother, you can probably tell he is a ball of energy. He is going to have many career options on Earth, but he must learn to stick to being his authentic self. He is outgoing, open minded, and a leader in providing motivational energy. He has many options, but those options will only become clear through embodying who he is. I see this is something that many of you on Earth experience. You think, think, think, without being. One thing that will never change is who you are on a soul level. Your soul is what anchors you into your body. Your body is what anchors you into your physical life.

When a soul is choosing their life purpose, firstly they look at the gifts they gained through their previous lifetimes. Some of these gifts are from what you could consider to be traumas that have been alchemized into something greater. For example, two lifetimes ago, I witnessed many females around me having complications specifically during childbirth. This prevented me from ever wanting children in that lifetime, out of fear. But then, in my next lifetime, I saw that there was a need on Earth for new ways of healing the body. So, as a combination of what Earth needed and what I experienced previously, I alchemized it into a gift. This gift allowed me to help others physically heal, which then dissolved my fear of having children in my previous lifetime, so I then deeply desired them.

I think it's often misunderstood that we need to conform to the normal structures of society in order to fulfill a purpose. However, for some, these structures work great for them! On Earth there are many different job roles that you can have, some more pleasurable and others requiring more labor, time, or grit. No job is better than the other, and the lessons learned from any job are what each soul chooses to experience. Some souls choose to run a business as a result of embodying their purpose. Some souls choose to work construction. Some choose to teach. The possibilities are endless. The bottom line is that a purpose fulfilled will look different for each soul.

That brings me to the discussion of fulfillment. Fulfillment feels like a complete cycle. No matter what needed to be done, you feel good about having done what was needed. Through how we each carry out our purpose, we are contributing to the betterment of the collective. We each need to do our part to raise the frequency on Earth.

As a human, you get to see the material form of the frequencies you feel and receive on a soul level. Calibrating to the frequency of your soul's purpose happens through embodying your authenticity. Then, as a result, you get to see the many options available to you. Earth specifically will challenge you to follow this path. The existence of things like free will have a part in influencing the path that you take towards your purpose. But, if you allow your soul to be the anchor for everything else, you will be able to carry out your purpose and feel fulfillment in this lifetime," she concludes.

Me: "Your wisdom is so appreciated! I can see how you and your brother are in the same soul family; you both carry such motivational and inspiring energy. Thank you!"

She nods her head in gratitude as her brother shows a picture of bright, glittering, rainbow lights to show his appreciation too.

Chapter 6: How a Spirit Baby Chooses Their Parents

The process of a soul choosing their parents is a journey filled with intent, and with the knowing that there are infinite possibilities existing within their decision. When a soul chooses their parents, they are trusting that their decision will benefit their soul growth, but are also stepping up to the plate with bravery in knowing that free will exists on Earth and they will be navigating their relationships with parents from human perspectives.

The excerpt you will be reading in this chapter is one that will require you to follow along with your imagination! The information I am channeling from the spirit baby realm is being delivered in images and video-like scenarios from the realm itself and what is transpiring for different souls right now as we speak.

A soul enters a space surrounded by other souls with whom they have been physically related to in previous lifetimes. They display feelings of comfortability around one another, expressing that they feel trusting of how each of them plays a role in each other's lives from one life to the next. At times, it is this scenario in which the souls will gather and simply choose to switch roles. These groups are called soul families. Soul families consist of souls that will continuously share lives with one another whether as family, friends, or important figures in each other's lives. The agreement that souls make for the way they will interact in their next lifetime is called a soul contract.

Let's switch gears now and talk about these contracts!

A soul is currently showing a piece of paper with a signature, which is representing the way we perceive contracts. They split the paper in half and are waving their fingers in a manner of, "No no no. Let me show you what a soul contract actually looks like!"

Another soul appears, and they show a cord of white light connecting them together through their solar plexus. (These souls are presenting themselves in human form to better show this process.) Energies are passing back and forth from one soul to another between the cord. These energies are showing up like a sound wave, and represent frequencies. The giving and receiving of these energies, and the agreement upon them, determines the 'contract.' Soul contracts are not set in stone and are malleable. They act more like a blueprint than a contract as we know it.

For example, a soul may create a soul contract with their parents when their parents are already in human form. Even in human form, at our core we are a soul who communicates with frequencies. While in our physical body, this is done unconsciously. If a parent communicates with their spirit baby on a concern such as desiring more time before conceiving, their soul contract may be altered.

Let's take a moment to pause with our imagination here and discuss a topic that comes up often and can be quite sensitive.

Many wonder how it is possible that a soul chooses their parents when there are unfortunate scenarios such as abuse that occur. People wonder how a soul could choose that, or why they chose it if it was something they experienced in their life. No soul can predict violence, abuse, etc. When a soul chooses their parents, they are fully aware of those parents' soul journeys, any wounding they may have in their current physical lifetime, as well as what they can learn from those parents. Unfortunately, as heartbreaking as it is to think of, acts of any form of abuse are a free will, human decision. No soul, no matter their frequency, or purpose, can influence the physical decisions and actions of a human being (nor can any human truly decide the decisions of another.) The souls are aware of the possibilities, but cannot make predictions. A soul is aware of wounding and trauma when choosing their parents, but they do not choose abuse. It is important to recognize whether you or someone you know have been in these instances to acknowledge the moral reality of the situation and seek the proper assistance.

The soul's process in choosing parents is evaluating what they can learn from them and use that knowledge to expand in their own growth. In scenarios like the one above, in our physical bodies the way that we would heal our trauma and grow is through getting to the root of the patterns and behaviors of those who influenced our lives, and how those were projected onto us. It is these roots, whether positive or negative, that a soul considers in choosing their parents.

Chapter 7: Spirit babies Incarnated as an Animal

I was in a client session with a woman who was seeking clarity around her previous miscarriages, and she shared a story of being afraid of dogs her whole life. On a family trip shortly after one of her miscarriages occurred, she felt a connection to a stray dog that her family adopted. She shared that it was as if her fear completely went away, and was curious as to if this dog was one of her spirit babies.

When I channeled from the soul of the spirit baby, it felt like part of them was communicating with me, while another part of them was present within this dog and the dog's life. The spirit baby shared with me that when a soul incarnates as an animal, their soul isn't fully in that animal's body. More intellectually advanced beings such as humans will have the majority of their soul within their body. Having most of our soul grounded into the body keeps us fully present on Earth while remaining connected to higher realms.

The spirit baby explained that when a soul inhabits the body of an animal, they can be aware of their physical senses and experiences, but are more aware of vibrations, other beings and entities, etc. The spirit baby went on to share that this reason was why my client felt so connected to this dog, while the spirit baby also being able to fluidly communicate telepathically and through my clairvoyance and clairaudience during the session.

Spirit babies will sometimes use animals as a way of

experiencing a simpler "in between" life to ease into their next lifetime as a human. Once a soul becomes a human, they are presented with the opportunities and responsibilities agreed upon before their lifetime. Humans have the intellectual awareness, and physical resources, to create groundbreaking change within the collective. Whether someone lives a "normal" life, or a life that may be considered adventurous or phenomenal, it takes bravery and courage for a soul to decide to come back to Earth as a human.

Animals are creatures that allow us to feel connected to home; home being God, Source, Universe, etc. Due to animals being more connected to higher levels of consciousness on a daily basis, they exude the vibrations of love and peace. If you own a pet, I am sure you can relate to the feeling of being unconditionally loved from them!

In the next chapter we're going to explore a simple yet effective way of asking your spirit baby to send a sign, or provide confirmation to a question, and strengthen your connection with them!

Chapter 8: Establishing the Connection - A Practice for Asking Your Spirit Baby for a Sign or Confirmation

Navigating the twists and turns of the path to conception often takes us to places beyond the physical. When reaching out to your spirit baby, the practice of asking for signs or confirmations can be a magical and deeply spiritual experience. Let's dive into this amazing method together:

Setting the Stage:
Picture a moment of quiet serenity, a cozy corner where you can be alone with your thoughts. Maybe light a candle, dim the lights, or weave in any personal rituals that make you feel connected and serene. This sacred space isn't just physical—it's a vessel for the energy that links you to your spirit baby.

Choosing the Sign:
Now, let's talk about the sign. It's not just any sign; it's something deeply personal and meaningful for you and your spirit baby. It could be a symbol, a song, a color—something that resonates with the unique story you're creating together. This sign becomes the language through which you communicate across realms. When I first began connecting with my spirit baby, I started out with choosing random signs that came to mind! One was a white butterfly. Another was a ladybug. Those are now two main ways that I know my spirit baby is around me! Don't overthink what to choose, just know what you choose will be used as part of your unique language with your spirit baby!

The 24-Hour Window:
Imagine setting the stage and then asking, "If you are here, send me a *sign of choice* within 24 hours." Why 24 hours?

Well, it's like creating a magical window—a time when the universe whispers back to you. It's not too long to be overwhelming, but long enough to let the magic unfold.

Interpreting the Signs:
As those 24 hours unfold, open your heart and senses. Signs may pop up in unexpected ways—a chance encounter, a dream that leaves you with a warm glow, or a series of perfectly timed coincidences. Trust your instincts, feel the energy, and be open to the little winks from your spirit baby.

Engaging in this dialogue with your spirit baby is like having a heart-to-heart across dimensions. It's a journey that deepens your connection, bringing comfort, guidance, and the sweet assurance that you're on this path together. So, with sincerity, openness, and a sprinkle of magic, embrace the mysterious and miraculous dance on the road to welcoming your little one into this world.

You can use this practice for reassurance, for yes/no guidance, or to provide a glimmer of positivity and magic to your day!

If the 24 hours go by and you don't receive a sign, try the practice with something different such as, "If it is in my highest good to go to "x" restaurant, place, etc. send me *sign of your choice." Doing this practice will allow you to develop your intuition and become receptive to the energy around you. We all have intuition, but just like any muscle, it takes strengthening and honing to be fully tapped in to its power and potential.

Part 2:

Spiritual
Fertility

Chapter 9: Why Some Pregnancies Are Planned, and Others are Not

A soul coming to Earth is always intentional. Yet, not all pregnancies are consciously planned. In some cases, using resources we have today like contraception fail. Is it simply an accident, or is there more than meets the eye when miraculous or unplanned pregnancies occur?

The image being shown to me is coming from the spirit baby realm as a collective. This seems to be a topic that they are passionate about, as they are displaying a highly vivid visual that feels like I am watching a movie in 4D.

They are taking me through microscopic images of the parts of a flower. They are emphasizing that everything in this flower was intentionally designed to work in harmony with external factors such as soil, sun, and water. Even though the flower is designed perfectly, the external factors can effect the health of the flower.

The spirit baby realm is saying that this relates to our experiences on Earth. On a soul level, we were designed intentionally and perfectly. However, the external factors around us can effect the trajectory of our health and overall quality of life. I feel called here to connect with one spirit baby so we can understand how to piece this together with events like planned and unplanned pregnancies.

As I am setting the intention for a soul to come forward, a

soul with a baby blue aura steps forward, surrounded by hundreds of other blue light beings of a smaller size. They begin to create a circular formation, rotating like a spiral meant to hypnotize you. The spirit baby of the bigger size comes forward.

I ask the spirit baby for insight onto the topic we are talking about today.

The spirit baby begins, "Ah yes, I can see why this would be something you are inquiring on. As a human it can be easy to look around you and constantly wonder why things are the way they are. When spirit babies choose to come to Earth, the timing they choose is based on what their soul, and their parents' souls, agreed upon. In the instances where a pregnancy was planned, the agreement between all of the souls was established long before the birth of the spirit baby's parents. In pregnancies that are unplanned, there is a rich history of shared past lifetimes, however there is an open possibility as to whether the souls will join each other in this lifetime. In unplanned pregnancies, there is no pressure or need for massive expanded growth for the souls to meet again, so when a spirit baby decides they want to come in, it is often an abrupt decision. It is like jumping off of a cliff without any hesitation. In the. physical world, this abrupt decision from the spirit baby manifests as shock, disbelief, or confusion in the mother, or both parents.

Time operates differently in the spirit baby realm. What a spirit baby sees as timing that is in alignment with what they desire, and what can be offered to the parents' souls through this experience, the parents may see this as a surprise.

When a spirit baby decides to make this abrupt decision, they understand there is a chance that the parents may not agree with their timing. In the physical, it may seem inconvenient and not something that they have room for currently.

The reason why a spirit baby will feel comfortable to go forth with the decision to rapidly jump in is because of the long history they already have with one or both of the parents they choose. (They may have a connection to more than 2 parents in cases like adoption where there are biological and adoptive parents.)

Spirit babies have a perspective that extends beyond our intuitive senses as human beings. They know that if a parent decides now is not the right time, and makes decisions following that, that they can still have the opportunity to live out their soul purpose in the future.

While spirit babies are aware of this, they are also not desensitized to the emotions that may come up in the parents. They feel all of these emotions, amplified. Spirit babies understand that the timing they are choosing to come in may cause turmoil in the parents' lives. The decision to abruptly come in is not done out of ill intent, but because of the desire to be reunited with members of their soul family.

Whatever transpires after a spirit baby comes in rapidly will be understood by the spirit baby. Spirit babies are operating at a higher consciousness than humans, and always have deep compassion and understanding for what souls who are already here are experiencing in their physical life."

I thank the spirit baby for joining us, and the spirit baby sends a glowing blue ball of light to share their appreciation for connecting.

Chapter 10: Grief, Loss, and The "Second Pregnancy"

I hesitated to write this chapter for the longest time, and I'm not one to procrastinate! You could say that my own experience of early pregnancy loss put a slight fear into the back of my mind on what would be channeled for this portion of the book... yet it is a topic that needs discussion, healing, and clarity. After the loss, I didn't feel the calling to sit in meditation with my spirit baby and figure out the 'why' behind what transpired.

Fast forward a few months later, while reminiscing on a recent conversation with a family member, I began to put puzzle pieces together in my mind that then revealed the 'why.'

It didn't feel overwhelming to understand it. In fact, it was a feeling of, "This makes sense now."

After having this realization and closure to my own experience, I finally felt open to be able to receive wisdom around topics of grief and loss from the spirit babies to help all that will be reading this book. This topic will be a conversation between me and my spirit baby.

As my fingers click along the keyboard, I am becoming aware of the feeling of loss. It's a feeling of loss of myself, as a result of the experience. I have not yet called in my spirit baby for this conversation, but have already heard the first ethereal hug of wisdom coming through for us which is, "It's okay to feel into the feeling of losing yourself. It's okay to feel like this is a death of yourself. You may never be the same, and that is okay."

Taking a deep breath, I am now connecting to my spirit baby to join us.

Initially going into this, I honestly felt anxious! Yet now being connected with my spirit baby, I feel a sensation of being elevated, as if my spirit baby's vibration is feeling into mine and lifting it up.

No matter where you are in your journey with your spirit baby, know that they can hold the emotions that you are feeling.

I begin to say to my spirit baby, "I have been hesitant to have this conversation, but now I feel ready. There are a lot of emotions I am feeling going into this, but I know that by having this conversation we are partaking in a beautiful act of service for the world. I'm not sure where exactly I want to take this conversation, but I trust you to lead the way."

My spirit baby has a zen yet prideful look on their face, as if we have met on vibrational terms, on a new level, that we have not before.

My spirit baby begins, "I applaud you for finally taking this step. For your own understanding, I knew that the time would come. You didn't need me to tell you, because you trusted in your own heart and intuition. When a woman experiences her spirit baby parting from her womb, her intuition is forever increased. Even though the spirit baby has left the womb, the energetic connection is still present.

In the presence of a spirit baby, your energetic state is instantly raised and cleansed. There is no other way for this connection with a spirit baby to occur. Spirit babies are naturally acting from the frequencies of love. Even in the moments where she is grieving, her spirit baby is still working. Her spirit baby may not be growing themselves in her womb, but they are growing a new version of her within herself.

Energetically, a second pregnancy occurs after a spirit baby leaves. This second pregnancy will often continue for the duration of 9 months just like in the physical. The combining of one soul, into the vessel of a human body through what we know as "pregnancy" initiates a new understanding of life and beyond what has been up until this point. Even when that physical pregnancy no longer exists through the growth of a human body, the essence of creation and birth will continue in the mother."

I let my spirit baby know, "Since you left my womb, I definitely have not felt the same. The time period that has since happened after has been a time of deep reflection.

I feel closer than ever to understanding my desires, and knowing what I want to manifest in life. It's like the mentality that I began to develop when you were here hasn't stopped. It's only grown. Does this period of growth apply to all circumstances of pregnancy loss? It would be beneficial if you could talk to us about what happens in various pregnancy loss scenerios."

My spirit baby continues, "No matter the situation, the 'second pregnancy' continues. When a spirit baby leaves they understand the repercussions of their decision. They know that as a result of their departure, lower frequency feelings like anger, pain, and grief will occur. This departure, however, is not something entirely under a spirit baby's control like how you may think. In the creation of a realm, space, or consciousness, energies of similar vibrations and frequencies are magnetized together. From there, they grow and expand. With pregnancy loss as a result of the spirit baby leaving on their own, it is because there is a stronger vibrational pull that they must tend to. To put it into a physical picture, this may be assisting another soul to the spirit baby realm, or the other way around. It could be that things have shifted on the Earth plane and that more time is needed before they come in. There is no, one reasoning behind each situation. This does not mean that the parent(s) weren't 'high vibe' enough, or didn't take care of themselves, etc. There is massive movement, change, and growth happening outside the 3D world that humans are mostly or entirely unaware of.

If someone intentionally chooses for their pregnancy to end, the spirit baby will still return to the spirit baby realm. The parent involved will still have the 'second pregnancy period' of growth. The majority of the time, a spirit baby will understand and come back at a time that is better for both that person and for themselves. In less common cases, they will choose another parent(s) if their purpose and energy is in alignment with what is happening on Earth, and the role that they will play in it.

Although choosing for your spirit baby to leave can be one that is incredibly painful emotionally, one of the most healing things that can be done is to create room for them (as comfortable as you are) for them to guide you spiritually and intuitively in your life. Even though it wasn't the right time physically, the spirit baby still has deep love and wisdom to offer. If it is not something that is desired, the spirit baby will understand.

This is something that I would advise to any scenario with pregnancy loss. You do not have to be meditating every day, or journaling, or pulling tarot cards if you are not comfortable doing so. However, a simple, "I am open to feeling you with me" can be a catalyst healing to occur.

It is also a good idea to energetically nurture yourself. After a pregnancy loss, it can feel like you are irritated, annoyed, or overwhelmed more often, sometimes out of nowhere. While the roller coaster of emotions can be a contributing factor, it is also because there is still an intertwining spiritual connection with your spirit baby. Not only have they been with you energetically, but they have now been within your body, and as part of you.

Setting the intention, doing an energy clearing, or communicating with your spirit baby on having a distinct separation between their energy and yours will help with this.

No matter what has happened, never forget to be human.

Spirit babies are eager to be a human, and also understand what that will entail.

Allow your tears to be the water that cleanses your mind.

Allow the longing to envelop you as a hug from the divine, because your desire to have this baby with you is from the highest and most loving frequencies.

Place your hand on your heart and feel it beating; making the connection that this pulse represents the pulsating energies all around. These are energies here to guide, support, and heal.

Whether you desire to sever the energetic connection to your spirit baby, or you desire to call them back in, be reminded of the miracle of your own creation, and of the creation around you. No matter what you choose, in whichever case, by following your heart you are making the right decision. Everything that we need and want already exists, and is simply changing and multiplying. It is unpredictable, and can feel like a void.

What if you felt beauty within that void?

What if the void where you feel the strong winds of your intuition, combined with the the rough waters of your grief, along with the taste of what lies ahead for you and your journey were an enlightening platter that only brought you closer to who you truly are on a soul level too?

Your spirit baby is always encouraging you to be true to this soul self within. They will guide you, whether within your womb or within the womb of this infinite universe."

I take a few moments to digest what was channeled, and thank my spirit baby.

If pregnancy loss is something that you have experienced, I encourage you before moving into the next chapters to take a few moments to imagine yourself in 'the void' picture shared by the spirit baby. If you haven't experienced loss, but are calling in your spirit baby to conceive, tailor the picture to what fits you.

If you feel called, use the journal prompts below as inspiration to work through the emotions coming up for you:

1.) By feeling my intuition as wind, what am I feeling called to do or surrender into?

2.) By feeling my grief as rough water, (or, insert another emotion) how can I self regulate through this?

3.) By feeling the beating of my heart, what am I inspired to put more attention into that is alive and ready to grow?

4.) What kind of energy or comfort would I like to receive from my spirit baby?

5.) In this current phase of my life, and based on my previous answers, what role would I like my spirit baby to play in my life currently? How do I desire for them to guide me?

Note: The "second pregnancy" also continues after a birth (whether vaginal or C-section.) We know this period as postpartum. A woman's mind and body will change even after the initial 9 month period after birth, however just like with loss, this is the time where the heart and intuition are fully burst open and initiate a new evolution for the woman. Men, too, experience a 9 month period of time after birth where they are called to show up differently and in more alignment with what their relationship and family need.

Chapter 11: The Energetics of the 1st Trimester

A recent realization I uncovered around the energy of the first trimester came following a video I saw of what it looks like when a new neural connection in the brain is formed.

To put it simply, a neural connection is a term describing the process of one cell communicating with another. When we learn new things, new neural connections are formed.

On average, it takes 90 days, (or 3 months), for a new neural connection to fully wire together.

3 months is also the length of the first trimester, and where we see women experiencing the majority of their symptoms and adapting to the new change happening within their body.

Spirit babies describe the process of coming into their physical body similar to how a neural connection is formed.

The visual coming through is of a young girl splashing in a lake, then coming out to dry off, then jumping back in!

I ask her to introduce herself.

"Hi! My name is Lily!"
She continues to show herself going back and forth between the lake and the dry land which is making me a little dizzy to be watching repeatedly in my mind's eye!

I ask her if she could take a break for a moment, and I see her emerge from the lake shivering a little bit but with a big smile on her face! I can physically feel the chill on her skin, and equally feel the joy she is displaying on her face.

As you may have noticed in the chapters so far, we always connect with the perfect spirit baby to discuss the topic with us! Lily has joined us because she is currently making her way to Earth and was demonstrating, in a visual we can understand, the soul's process of going back and forth between the body.

She says, "I'm coming to my Mommy in 7 months! I have been throwing her for a bit of a loop with all of this moving around I am doing. I like to pop into my body for a split second, then connect back with all of my friends in the Realm, then come back to my Mommy. I am always connected to her, but it seems when i get to her womb I always push up energy out of her body that she doesn't need anymore."

I am shown a picture of a woman vomiting which is not a pretty picture at all! But Lily reassures us that the symptoms that come with pregnancy are a reflection for the spirit baby's gifts and purpose. "Unfortunately," Lily continues, "Because our frequency is so high, when we come to the womb there is no choice but for anything lower frequency to be completely removed from the body!"

She splays her arms out to display the *large* amount of energetic purging that comes with the first trimester.

"We play a role in the sperm meeting the egg. A miraculous feat by that could only be accomplished by something that's higher frequency than a human!"

She gives a cheeky smile.

"For a little bit, we are like scientists because we are creating the vessel that will get us to Earth. It's like building your own car! We firstly begin to connect the 'identity' part of our soul into the embryo. This is the energy of 'I am' and moving from being a pure energy to being physical. From that point forward, we will always have the memory of the womb, or even sometimes a lab nowadays, where conception happened. We will have this memory regardless of if we come Earthside or not. Even the smallest or faintest of memories will have an influence in our journey to Earth, and even future lifetimes.

Then, we create an energetic cord between our physical body and our soul. Our soul can be in multiple places at once, so our physical body just becomes a place that we can anchor into!"

Lily shows me a visual of tossing a rope from a boat to a dock so it can be tied around a cleat and keep the boat in a secure position.

She continues, "We will come and go as we please. The womb is like another universe to us. It would be like if you, being from Earth, went to Mars. You are still alive and you are still aware, but it is literally an entire different world. It can shock you at first! That is why we spend some time floating in and out of our physical body. When I describe us coming and going, that doesn't mean our physical body is empty space. Think of the rope and how even when it is tied up to something else, it is still connected to the boat.

This is also the time where we try to be the biggest cheerleader for the person carrying us!

Energetically, we are taking you on a ride on a rocket ship with no prior training, knowledge, or precaution!

The body needs time to adjust to what your soul is feeling, so it sends signals to you through 'pregnancy symptoms'.

However, just know that you are returning to your natural state of being. The vibration you are ascending to while pregnant is the vibration that you held all the time before coming into your physical body.

Going 'home" can seem stressful, but your spirit baby is your right hand man (or woman!) You can ask your spirit baby to be in your presence and anchor into your womb when things feel overwhelming or tiring. They will also never deny spending moments that are exciting with you!

Some spirit babies don't stay past the first trimester.

Every spirit baby will have their reasons; they perceive something on the horizon that you can't right now and they leave, there was an energetic upgrade they wanted you to have that didn't require fully birthing, etc. It's important to connect with your spirit baby and they will be able to give you clarity!"

I thank Lily for taking a moment to talk to us. She smiles wide and (energetically) gives me a hug, then returns back to playing in the lake.

Chapter 12: The Energetics of the 2nd Trimester

A baby's physical senses begin to develop within the second trimester. Smell is the first sense that a baby will gain, beginning as early as 13 weeks. By the end of the second trimester, a baby will be able to open their eyes.

The second trimester is an exciting time where a mother will feel more settled into her body, as well as the spirit baby!

"Paisley" is the name of the spirit baby we are connected with in this chapter. She is taking me for a fast-paced adventure in my mind's eye, guiding me behind her as she runs through vast fields of flowers. Her energy is liberating and alive.

I ask her, "What is the rush? We are moving so quickly!"

She replies, "Yes, we are! This is what it starts to feel like for a spirit baby in the second trimester. The senses a spirit baby has before coming into the physical body is different from what is felt IN a body."

Paisley guides me in my mind's eye to an empty patch of grass where she invites me to sit with her while she takes a much needed breather!

She continues, "Listen to the wind. Feel the wind. You can't control it, or change it, or manipulate it. Sure you have tools and machines to direct it, but you can never control it.

A spirit baby, outside of a body, is like the wind; ever flowing, ever changing, and in many places at once. When the physical body continues to form, and the energetic cord gets stronger, the 'wind' starts to decrease. There isn't as much to-and-fro movement. Now the baby begins to FEEL the wind. We can imagine feeling this wind as becoming acclimated to the physical senses."

I process the metaphor she explained and say to her, "It's interesting because it seems like a soul, who is a spirit baby, gets to BE the wind whereas once they come into a physical body, they FEEL the wind. In essence, is this a reflection for feeling the energy of themselves? Do we all do this even after being born and growing up?"

"Precisely," she confirms, "The second trimester is all about the fusion of the astral and the physical. Everything outside of you is a manifestation of where you came from, and the many energies and particles in this universe that made you YOU. In the second trimester, with this new shift in the spirit baby's perception of the world developing around them, they begin to adapt to the new identity of being a stationary being with the ability to feel, rather than be felt."

Paisley places her hand to her heart and takes a deep breath in.

"This," she notes, referring to the deep breath with her hand on her heart, "Is something souls beg to feel. Becoming a human is a privilege. In other astral groups and civilizations, your energy can be bent, shifted, and manipulated. There's a sense of control. Humanity requires surrender. It is the brave soul who will choose to become something, someONE who is the receiver of the feelings, the experiences, and energies."

We take a moment to pause. I ask her, "If this experience is something that is solidified in the second trimester, how as a spirit baby are you able to demonstrate messages and feelings that you supposedly don't feel?"

"We feel it ALL," she says, "But we are the conductor of it. We are our own being, yet intertwined with everything all at once. Humanity provides separation, while still being connected to the Source. When a soul decides that they want to come to Earth, they begin to learn how to surrender and separate, especially since they will be decreasing their baseline frequency. It's like training to use a parachute, or regulate your breathing as a plane descends."

I nod to her with understanding.

From there she shares, "The second trimester for a spirit baby feels like a dream for a human. When you dream, it is a fantasy but it is also reality because your mind is coming up with symbols and people to give you messages. Even though what you are being shown isn't actually happening, sometimes you still have your physical senses within the dream. it feels the same for a spirit baby, except the dream is actually reality. It feels a bit hazy, but not so much to where the spirit baby's physical body isn't alert. Even though when you talk to your baby in the womb it may physically sound like an echo, because the spirit baby still has some of their energy in the astral, they will be able to feel the frequency itself of what you said and react to that.

Image if there is a car that is a bit distant from you. You can hear the person in the car is playing music, and even though you don't understand the lyrics that are playing, by hearing the beat echoing from the car you can make a pretty good guess as to what kind of music they are listening to!

The energetic cord in the second trimester is like an anchor with a rope attached to a boat. The spirit baby is like a scuba diver, still moving around in the vastness of the astral, but the energetic cord (or the anchor and the rope) are in view to guide the baby back to the boat (their physical body!)

Babies start kicking their legs in the second trimester. See, I didn't show you quick moving legs in the beginning for no reason!

The kicking of the legs is a physical expression of the energetic momentum and changes that are happening as they shift back and forth to being mainly in the astral, or mainly in the physical. At this point however, there will be a solid attachment to the physical body even if the spirit baby is still connecting with lots of energies in the astral."

I ask Paisley how a mother can connect with her baby in the second trimester with all of the changing energies that are happening!

She advises, "Anything you feel in your physical body is a guide. If you notice you feel a bit dizzy, or have a headache, or even simply feel lighter that day, a more spiritual practice to connect with your baby will be beneficial. So if you are feeling this way, meditation will definitely be a go-to!

If you are feeling heaviness or sensations anywhere below your waist, it would be good for you to connect with your baby through intuitive eating, playing a frequency soundtrack, or gently rubbing your stomach to comfort your spirit baby.

A baby will always be born from a lower energy center, whether C-section or vaginal birth. So while pregnant when you feel a lot of energy higher up in your body, it is your spirit baby connecting with higher frequencies, energies, and dimensions. When you feel energy lower in your body, your baby is more rooted to their physical body. This is also a physical representation of the transition of the spirit baby's frequency going from a baseline of 700+ hz to a baseline of 200. Although, this baseline frequency for humans is beginning to slowly raise and most babies nowadays are taking on a baseline frequency of around 300hz."

In my mind's eye I see Paisley smile. I can tell that, while we still energetically sit together in the open patch of grass, she will highly value peace and space coming into her next lifetime. I can feel the euphoria emanating from her soul.

"Paisley, it has been a pleasure! Thank you so much for

taking me to this space that you love and spending time with me."

Paisley says humbly, "You're welcome" and I close out our conversation.

Chapter 13: The Energetics of the 3rd Trimester & Birth

I'd like to take you through a grounding practice with me before channeling this next chapter. This chapter is being written outside, (in the shade because the heat of the 95 degree weather will distract me!) in a spot that is allowing the breeze to come over me. Whether you are inside or outside, I invite you to stare up at the sky. If it is a sunny day, that is a bonus! Just make sure not to stare directly at the sun! Be present with the light, and the way it is allowing you to view all of the life around you. While we may see the other realms and dimensions as being "up there" in the sky, they merge right here right now with our current reality. While looking up at the sky may invite you to think about the vast universe that exists beyond our planet, it is also a reminder of the miracle of life that we have here.

It is THIS life that our spirit baby is choosing. It is THIS body that our spirit baby is seeing as a safe haven to dwell in as a vessel bringing them to Earth.

Place your hand on your womb, and repeat with me,
"Life exists within my body."
"The creation around me is proof that I, too, can create life."
"Nobody will experience the world like I do, and that is a gift."
"I am thankful for the spirit baby that is choosing me, and trusting me, with giving them this life."

I am also now taking a moment to do the energetic practice from Chapter 2 before channeling.

I am greeted by a soul named "Percy" who approaches into my energy field with a calm energy, but one that feels like descending. It feels like if you were to jump into a pool, but in slow motion. He takes my attention away from the sky, and brings it to the ground.

I say to him, "Hi Percy! I believe you have already begun to show us what the third trimester feels like, as we can tell by the energy of descending that you are showing us! Is that feeling uncomfortable for a spirit baby?"

"Hello, and it is an honor to be here. No, it is not uncomfortable at all! In fact, the role of the first and second trimester is to make this descension possible. Spirit babies become incredibly excited, because they know they are on their way to their destination! At this point in the pregnancy, the spirit baby has become accustomed to being in their body inside the womb. Except, they still retain all of the memories of their previous lifetime, the information of their purpose, and easy access to other realms and dimensions. However, once they are birthed into the world, they begin a slow process of forgetting these facts about their soul. The third trimester is the perfect time for the parents to do 'touch up' meditations with their spirit baby; asking them questions like, 'What makes you feel supported?' and 'How can I help you achieve your goals in this lifetime.'

Spirit babies also highly encourage mothers to trust themselves throughout the third trimester. The anticipation of the baby's arrival grows stronger, which can bring up fears, doubts, or worries within the parents. However, these are things your spirit baby can best help you with in the third trimester. They want you to feel empowered, safe, and secure. A practice you can do to feel safe in your body, and get energy moving around your aura as you get closer to birth, is to see a blue spiral of energy swirling around your root chakra, then extending it up to your head to create a cylinder shape, and moving your hips in circles as you wind the spiral higher."

I try the practice myself, and see how much of a relief it feels on the body!

Percy continues, "From there, stretch your legs in any way that feels comfortable. One of the best positions is on your hands and knees and parting your knees to open up the hips. During this stretch, visualize the same blue spiral expanding and stretching. We want to remind your body that, just like this energy, it can expand and stretch. Your energy is expanding and stretching with this new era of having a baby, and your body will physically stretch and expand to allow your body to birth your baby. The blue spiral also creates a safe vortex in your aura that you can come back to whenever you feel like tension needs to be released in the body.

From a spirit baby's perspective, they feel like they have held you in the first trimester, second trimester, and even before conception. They have always been there to hold space for you energetically, even if you could not feel it. They were always there, in the background. In this stage of pregnancy, you can now feel THEM more than ever. The third trimester is a celebratory time for a spirit baby. They see it as the beginning of them 'handing the torch' to you and you now being the one to support them, rather than the other way around. If there is one thing a spirit baby is sure of during the third trimester, is that as their easy access between realms and dimensions slowly closes, it begins to open up more for the mother.

If you need the rest, take it. If there is something specific you feel like you need to eat, follow that urge. It's not just your body signaling you to do these things, it's your higher self (the part of you with information for what is best for you) sending you messages.

Imagine two bars on a graph being displayed in a video. The bar that is taller represents your spirit baby and their frequency, while the bar that is lower represents you and your frequency. As pregnancy goes, on, the two bars heighten and shorten until they match up. Once they match up, this is when labor begins! With you and your spirit baby being on the same frequency, now it is a collaborative effort ot bring your spirit baby to Earth. It requires your presence, surrender, and safety as well as the spirit baby's."

I ask Percy to pause as I say to him with a giggle, "I wasn't expecting to get into the energetics of labor in this chapter but I am loving it! Please continue"

He goes on, "For a spirit baby, they can see the energy of the birth visually. Throughout labor, they see and feel themselves blasting through a rapidly moving spiral. The spiral looks like one that you may see in a hypnosis video, except it is much more colorful! This spiral is like a realm within itself. We can call this 'the birth realm." No other soul or spirit will occupy this realm other than the spirit baby and the helpful energies of other souls around them of their choosing. Not every spirit baby's journey through the birth realm will look the same. When the spiral appears to be a deep blue, with tinges of green, it signals a clear path. When colors of red, black, or orange appear, it slows down the birth process. These colors will come up based on the mother's emotions and any energies the mother may need to clear during birth.

Because birth is such a powerful process, many unconscious perceptions or old energies may come up for one or both parents. Understanding the existence of the birth realm can help a mother set intentions to clear energies coming up that will not serve her during birth.

Sometimes a spirit baby's baseline vibration will still be high enough to easily clear any blocks the mother is feeling. Other times, a different approach to the birth or medical intervention may be necessary. This doesn't mean something is 'wrong' with the mother or the baby, this just means that the energy coming up that is preventing ease has manifested to a degree where modern technology is needed and can help.

Babies born via C-section will be more inclined to remember previous lifetimes, their soul gifts, etc. because they didn't fully pass through the birth realm.

these babies will also, however, need a little encouragement to be grounded in this life because they will want to live in their mind and imagination a lot!

Babies who fully pass through the birth realm will still be able to access their soul gifts, purpose, etc. throughout their life, however a quicker process of experiencing amnesia to these will begin.

The birth realm is an entanglement of space and time. Your spirit baby is moving from the spirit baby realm where one moment to them may be a day for us, to an entirely different concept of time and space.

Vaginal birth also familiarizes the spirit baby with gravity, which is something that effects time and space. For C-section babies, they do not become familiar to the same degree which is why their main point of consciousness, or awareness, will be higher in the body. They are more likely for their consciousness to mainly rest in the third eye, or in their head, rather than in their heart, solar plexus, or stomach.

Birth is a life changing and magical experience! When you want to see your spirit baby's birth realm during labor, come back to your blue spiral, then intend for that to broadcast an image in your third eye of your spirit baby's birth realm.

Essentially, you want to see your blue spiral acting as a projector and giving you a view into your spirit baby's birth realm. If you see the colors that were mentioned, you can intend for them to be cleansed with a white light. As you see the white light cleansing the birth realm, visualize yourself breathing it in and filling your womb."

Before responding to Percy, I want to take a moment to acknowledge how powerful this is!

I bring my attention to Percy.

"Percy, what you have shared today is life changing. Women around the world are going to feel empowered knowing they can energetically help their spirit baby during birth, and take care of themselves in the process. I am so grateful to have connected with you, thank you!"

Percy says "You're welcome" and I see the outline of his energy fading from view in my third eye.

Chapter 14: The Way of the Womb

Some sources say that the universe is the womb of the divine mother. The divine mother is said to be the feminine aspect of the Creator. If we pretend for a moment that this is true, we can come to the conclusion that having the womb inside of our body also harnesses not just the power to create human life, but materialization of multiple forms of life.

My personal fascination with this concept began in 2021. At the time I wanted to rekindle my relationship with manifestation. This was happening at the same time I was exploring how the use of yoni eggs and yoni wands benefited women's energetic and physical health. I had overcome my battle with excruciating period pain and PMS, and was starting to experience pain-free cycles. (I still experience it to this day!) Now that I felt I had grown a healthy relationship with my womb and my cycle, I wanted to expand on my knowledge further.

In my intuition's classic language, I heard the whisper to channel my own manifestation practice. Yes, I visualized and did some light breath work like many other practices, but I did not expect to be led to involve my womb in the process.

It felt like I didn't have to question any of the next steps, as I watched what I was visualizing condense into a ball that entered my third eye, drifted down my body, and stopped in my womb. I could feel the intensity rising with each breath.

It was as if my desire had found a home within my body, and I was giving it the room to be as grand as it wanted to be.

Then, I visualized my body birthing this desire out into the universe, and I felt immersed in an entirely different universe. After opening my eyes, it felt like I had spent some time thinking of a memory rather of something that hasn't happened yet.

That was when I was ovulating.
Two weeks later, what I visualized came to fruition.
I did it again the next month.
Again, two weeks later, what I visualized happened.

Some things I visualized were simple; a couple of new clients, or a conversation with someone that I wanted to have.

Other things were life changing, like manifesting a house in a crazy market where it didn't look like we'd find a house within the budget, location, and standards we had.

I got engaged two weeks after doing this practice too!

I had a light-bulb moment when I realized that two weeks is also the average period of time between when a woman ovulates and then she finds out she is pregnant.

This chapter is going to speak to you if you have been doubting your power. Your ability to carry human life does not determine your worth, because you were born with a gift to shape your reality as you please. No matter your path to calling in your children, or how you had your children if they are Earthside with you, your womb is a powerhouse center of your body.

Even if, physically, your womb feels or has felt like she is letting you down, you came from a womb. A womb brought you here, and you have one within you too! Despite our physicality, we can tap into the essence of the Womb at any time. The womb represents creation, sensuality, and intuition.

She will let us know when something is a "yes."
She will let us know when something is off.
Our womb is like the best friend that doesn't sugar coat anything.
Sometimes what she expresses is uplifting and joyful. Other times, it may be harsh and triggering, but honest.

Women have what I like to call an "intuition circuit." This circuit is an exchange of energy connecting the womb, to the heart, then to the third eye. Then the third eye cycles the energy back to the womb to repeat the process.

Let's do a short practice together to bring some connection to the womb. As women, we oftentimes don't pay attention to our womb unless we are on our period. However, our womb is constantly shifting. Also, the more connected we are to our womb, the more we are able to feel our intution

working through our womb.
If you have had your uterus removed, you can set the intention for a white ball of light in your lower abdomen to represent the portal of the Womb.

Firstly, let's ensure to connect to the golden light from Source, and the pink light from the Earth. (We learned this in Chapter 2!)

Now, let's take some deep breaths.
Breathe in for 3 counts, then exhale for 4.
Now breathe in for 4 counts, hold it for 2, then exhale for 6.
Inhale for 6 counts, hold it in for 2, then exhale for 8.

Feel free to sigh, moan, or use your voice in any way that feels natural to you as you exhale.

Next, visualize an emerald green ball of light coming down from Source and stopping at your thighs.

As you breathe in, gently squeeze your pelvic floor as you visualize pulling the green ball of light up to your womb. Instead of the ball just traveling up to the womb, see the light being stretched as you pull it in.

The pelvic floor is a group of muscles that support the bladder, uterus, and bowel.

On the next breath, stretch the green light into your heart chakra. On this one, though, concentrate on only using the muscles in your yoni.

Next, stretch the green light up to your third eye.

Come back to a normal breathing pattern and see the green light floating back down to your thighs.

As you continue with this practice, you can circle your hips, roll out your neck, and move your body in any way that feels liberating and like a release to you.

Some of us have grown up being told to suck in our stomachs.
Some of us felt shameful about our periods.
Some of us have felt furious at our body and our womb.

Yet, she holds it all. She holds our juiciness and our turn on, AND our pain, shame, and grief.

What 3 things can you be grateful to your womb for today?

I'll go first:
I am grateful I can feel my womb twinging to let me know I am ovulating.
I am grateful for my womb and belly relaxing to allow me to breathe deeper.
I am grateful that my womb regulates and shifts throughout the month, without my conscious effort.

You can come to this practice whenever you are craving to

feel at home in your body, and take time to be present with yourself.

For the rest of the chapter, one of my spirit babies will be deciphering the energy of the womb and the role it plays in the spirit baby's journey to Earth:

"A womb is a portal between two worlds. It's the train that we can get on and off as we have our energy in two different worlds, two different dimensions, and two different ways of being. The womb is the cozy swaddle that keeps the spirit baby safe. It is not a dark and lonely place where we wait to come into the world. It's a time machine. People on Earth want time machines, but we already have them in the form of the womb.

Inside the womb, a spirit baby is nurtured energetically and physically. So much and so little is happening all at once. When the womb holds a spirit baby, its energy expands throughout the entire body.

Typically, any emotions or energies the womb holds will stay in the womb and come out through the menstrual cycle. During pregnancy, the energies and emotions spread throughout the entire body. If you feel nauseous, or emotional, you can set the intention for this energy to be washed away from you with a white light from Source. Then, you can set the intention for the energy that was washed away to blow up into blue light.
The womb is the closest entity a spirit baby has to their

original "home." In the womb, everything is magnetizing, joining, and multiplying. The womb, besides the brain, is the closest thing in the body to the universe. Many have not learned this in their lifetime. But if you are reading this, and you are learning, may I ask you, how would you treat and care for your womb as if it were the entire universe that encompasses you?

The womb may be a universe inside of you, rather than outside of you, but it is a universe.

You were gifted this by Source. You may have had your doubts, struggles, and experiences, but what if your Womb, like the Universe around you, needed just a few slight tweaks to intertwine energy and reflect the amazing result to you in your body?

A spirit baby will always find a home in the womb. While the womb is a portal, it is also a messenger between the parent and the growing baby. The womb is such a powerful container of energy that a parent can't NOT pay attention to it when it is growing, expanding, and growing life.

Bringing life into the world is designed to be a conscious process. The womb stretching and expanding is meant to stretch and expand YOU. This is not a daunting task, but rather an energy you harness within.

If your spirit baby is growing in someone else's womb, you can extend a white energetic cord between your womb and your spirit baby. Even though physically they are not in your body, energy has no bounds. They can use the energetic cord to intuitively connect with you through your womb, and to send you feelings within your womb so you can feel their presence. There are so many different ways for parents to become parents! Whether your own womb is growing your baby or not, it is still connected to the universe all around, and the one it has established within."

Chapter 15: Star Seeds

Science tells us that the odds of being born are 1 in 400 trillion. If you have ever pondered the phenomenon of miracles occurring, recognize that your life IS one.

While the scientific research tells us how rare it is to be here on Earth, spirit babies are chomping at the bit to come in.

It may take two to tango, but it takes three to establish an entirely new person's existence and reality.

We've learned an abundance of information on spirit babies' journeys, and the womb, but we have yet to cover the energetics behind what spirit babies denote the equivalent of shooting stars in the sky; the sperm.

There are more shooting stars throughout the universe that we are unaware of, but when we see that ONE that lights up the sky, what do we often say to each other?

"Make a wish."

Your life, was your soul's wish.
And it was made possible by one egg, and one sperm, fusing together to open a portal and allow YOU to come in.

In my third eye's view, a soul going by the name Ammon shines incredibly bright, with an energy that seems larger than life. Witnessing his energy is like being mesmerized by the sun creating rainbows as its light passes through surfaces.

Ammon's spirit is very quiet, but is offering to show us his display of energy for our exploration into the masculine side of conception.

He presents himself in human form cloaked in gold, as he spans his arms out beneath him to release a collection of sparkles. The sparkles represent the energy of the sperm, and what is activated within them.

"The sparkles," he says, "represents the millions of realities that can come to fruition."

Some sparkles immediately disappear. Others glow brighter and brighter, and continue to move quicker and quicker until it seems that they are buzzing.

Ammon shares, "Some realities aren't meant to be right now, in your view of the world. Some realities are more aligned with your soul, and your spirit baby's path."

Since Ammon is sharing the energetics of sperm through using sparkles, we will continue to refer to the energy and journey of the sperm as sparkles throughout this chapter.

One of the sparkles begins to outshine the rest, and as it expands, it presents what looks like a TV. What is shown here gives the spirit baby a glimpse into the reality, and all of the realities *within* that reality, for them. Ammon shows what happens if the spirit baby does in fact decide to move forward. The sparkle forms into the shape of a ring with the gaping opening being a portal for the spirit baby to be conceived.

The sparkle ring then condenses, and shoots in a random direction into thin air that is no longer seen. How could it be? A new life has been created. The energy wasn't destroyed. It just. changed. forms.

Ammon begins to speak, and even though he is a spirit baby, his voice sounds low with an echo. "A man who desires a child must decide if he is willing to be moved. The energy of his current reality, his thoughts, his beliefs, and his reflections will be passed on to the spirit baby. You do not have to be perfect. Some things your spirit baby is willingly choosing to take on and learn. You most likely desire stability when wanting to bring in a child. You must also, however, be willing to be moved by Source. Not all of the answers will be part of you immediately. That is why, you need to listen."

I ask Ammon to clarify what he means by "moved." He explains it as the willingness to be guided and to welcome in the new change that will happen.

Ammon lifts his arms and stretches them wide, so that his chest is directed upwards as he takes a long, deep breath. He explains, "A man must be open to possibility. When he allows himself to feel no hope, no optimism, or that things are a dead-end, the portals to the realities that lie ahead begin to close. The sperm is a tool for allowing those realities to make themselves known; one of those realities being the welcoming of a child. Man grants the wish of the spirit baby choosing to come. This does not mean he is not more powerful than Woman or Womb, but that he is the initiator of the opening of the portal, and Womb is the breath that solidifies and welcomes the spirit baby into its path through developing into new, human life.

The egg within the Womb is the destination at the end of the portal; the closing of one chapter and the beginning of another."

He smiles wide, and I feel the sensations of freedom that he radiates.

Whether the sperm and the egg meet in the womb, or out of the womb, the memories, beliefs, and experiences of the person they are from are contained within. Energy transcends time as we know it. It is not bound by the things we can clearly physically see or hold in the world around us. It is all connected, and the spirit baby infuses the Soul DNA of both parents, through the sperm and the egg, into the experience of their physical body.

Ammon says, "To bring a child into the world is an ambitious task. Yes, they have chosen you. For all of the fathers to be in the world, remembering that is the most empowering revelation of all. Can you trust in your ability to begin the process of welcoming them in? Do you feel unsure, but are willing to be guided? While your spirit baby is in the cosmos, preparing for their arrival, how can you be the shooting star they see that lights up their heart and grants their wish of coming to Earth? The power you have within your body to create life is not scary, but a gift to give for a soul that is going to light up the world with their essence. Don't hide your heart. Crack it wide open. Infuse the reality you plan to give to your spirit baby with the deepest amount of love and unwavering faith. They are already grateful."

Closing my eyes, I take a moment to thank Ammon for empowering the men out there who desire to be fathers. He closes his eyes, and I see his golden light become smaller as he disappears from view.

Chapter 16: Embracing Diverse Paths: Insights on Untraditional Journeys to Parenthood

Our souls have been weaving their way into the world since the dawn of humanity, yet our paths to coming Earthside are ever-evolving, and never carved in stone.

Though I believe we will one day find cures for infertility, the field of reproductive health has already paved new paths to parenthood that go beyond the traditional route.

In the intricate dance of life and spiritual journeys, conception is more than a physical process; it is a sacred agreement between souls made long before the moment of birth. These soul contracts, or blueprints, as we learned in a previous chapter, outline the roles that various souls will play in the life of a new being. This chapter delves into how these contracts manifest in different forms of conception, including adoption, surrogacy, sperm donation, IVF, IUI, and how spirit babies navigate these paths to find their way into the physical world. We will also explore the spiritual bonds formed with step-parents, who play an essential role in a spirit baby's journey.

Adoption and the Soul's Journey
Adoption is a beautiful example of how soul blueprints extend beyond biological connections. The agreement between a spirit baby and adoptive parents is forged in the spiritual realm, before birth, as a possibility. The spirit baby may choose to be conceived by one set of parents, but knows that

another family has another strong likelihood be the one to raise them. Most spirit babies establish connections with their biological parents even before their parents are born. However, part of the process involves evaluating *multiple* families and soul connections to choose who will bring them Earthside. For spirit babies who are adopted, not only did they choose their biological parents, but also possible 2nd and 3rd sets of families if the biological parent chooses to follow through on the path of placing the baby for adoption. Spirit babies make this decision based on the biological parents' soul journey, where they are energetically at the time of conception, and how they are approaching their feelings around the pregnancy. The decision to create a connection with a different family, other than the biological parents, will come while the other family(ies) are *already incarnated* on Earth.

If the child is placed for adoption as a toddler through young adult, their higher self will begin calling in parental figures just as their soul did before conception, except while already on Earth. Our higher self is the part of us that is the embodiment of the most aligned, fulfilled, version of ourselves.

This agreement hinges on the life lessons and spiritual growth that all parties—biological parents, adoptive parents, and the baby—are meant to experience. This divine arrangement is not random, but is part of a larger spiritual blueprint that guides the souls involved toward their destined encounters and lessons.

If you have adopted, or are thinking of adopting, you are not your child's 'second' choice. You are the *best* choice their soul, and your soul, made.

A spirit baby choosing adoptive parents is like making a last minute change to a dance routine in a show right before the curtain comes up, but it adds something extra special that brings tears to the audience's eyes. Your higher self, and your child's, went to work unconsciously to bring you into each other's lives, and it has (or will) create an abundance of love in the family you are destined to raise.

Surrogacy and Sperm Donation

In surrogacy and sperm donation, the spirit baby often has a strong cord connection with one of the intended parents. We learned in previous chapters that a spirit baby creates a cord between their soul and their physical body. Spirit babies also establish cords with intended parent(s). We can be corded into anything; other people, media, entities, situations, etc. Learning how to cut cords daily is amazing for our energetic hygiene! It resets our energy, and prevents us from feeling symptoms like fatigue and irritation as a result of the cords. With our spirit babies, however, we want to place our attention towards strengthening the cord since it helps them ease into the journey of going from soul to human. Being corded into only 1 intended parent allows the baby to give their parent the freedom to choose how they wish to bring them into the world. Whether through surrogacy or another method, the spirit baby remains dedicated to joining their chosen parent, honoring the soul contract that has been in place since before conception.

A surrogate plays a vital role in this spiritual journey, offering her body as a vessel for the spirit baby while sharing her own soul's lessons and energy. A spirit baby will not acquire DNA-based soul lessons, however they will take on emotion-based lessons and attributes. Many spirit babies born through surrogacy will have a tendency to be charitable, highly empathetic, and in tune with other people's needs.

The surrogate will be the baby's first physical introduction to the world around them, and it is important for the surrogate to be intentional with nervous system regulation, boundaries, and the main environments she will be in while pregnant.

Sperm donation adds another layer to the spiritual journey of conception. The baby acknowledges that their journey will involve acquiring DNA lessons from the sperm donor. The difference between DNA-based lessons, and lessons that a spirit baby chooses based on past lifetimes, their purpose, etc. is that the DNA-based lessons are connected to lineages with memories of experiences that have passed from one generation to the next through the body. Instead of the DNA lessons being taken on intentionally like the others, it is known that these lessons are part of the acquisition of that specific DNA. The spirit baby integrates these lessons into their life, adding depth and complexity to their spiritual and physical existence.

Spirit babies who are conceived via a sperm donor may take on characteristics of wanting to create sustainable change in the world, and 'building an empire', so to speak, if their soul wants to take an entrepreneurial route as part of their soul purpose.

The spirit baby integrates these lessons into their life path, contributing to their overall spiritual evolution. The involvement of multiple souls in the process of conception enriches the spirit baby's experience, allowing them to navigate their earthly journey with a broader perspective and deeper understanding.

IVF and IUI

In vitro fertilization (IVF) is a powerful method of assisted reproduction that opens a unique spiritual portal. When an embryo is created, it acts as a beacon for spirit babies. Not all spirit babies who come through this portal are meant to be birthed to the intended parents. This portal is a gateway, and invites in spirit babies who are corded into their parents, AND other spirit babies who may just be curious but have no connection to the parents. Only those with a deep, intentional connection to the parents will strengthen their cord to the embryo and continue the journey into physical life. The creation of multiple embryos in IVF allows spirit babies to choose the best-suited vessel for their journey. Even though some spirit babies who come through the portal don't have a connection with the intended parents, they can still cord into one or multiple embryos. The difference with this cord is that it was created by interacting with the embryo, but has no connection to the parents. It is possible for a spirit baby to be corded into multiple embryos, from multiple people, at once. Imagine it like a bee pollinating multiple flowers.

When this occurs, it is because they don't have a soul agreement with any of the parents. A spirit baby who has a soul agreement with the parents will *only* be corded into embryos created *by* those parents. A spirit baby who desires to be born to the intended parents can cord into multiple embryos at once from those parents.

Cutting cords between spirit babies who attach to embryos with no intention of being with those parents allows them to create soul agreements and attachments quicker with parents who are the best fit to bring them Earthside.

If a spirit baby who does not have a soul agreement with the intended parents is corded into an embryo at the time of embryo transfer, they will simply leave. (You can still cut the cord to ensure their soul journey is not being hindered from their interaction with your embryo.)
With any cord cutting practice, it is also imperative to practice energetic shielding for yourself and your spirit baby no matter how they are conceived. In the next page, you will be taken through a general cord cutting practice. You do not need to worry about your spirit baby becoming disconnected. You can set the intention that they will remain corded into you.

General cord cutting method that you can do for you and/or your spirit baby:

1.) Connect yourself to the golden light from Source and the pink light from the Earth

2.) Visualize a giant white dome representing your electromagnetic field. If you are doing the energy work on yourself, see a hologram of your body 6 inches away from your physical body (within the sphere)

3.) Set the intention to call down the light bodies of any person, situation, entity, or object that you are corded into.

4.) See the light bodies 12 feet away from your hologram/light body. Light body is an interchangeable term for aura.

5.) See the light bodies being corded into a translucent lava lamp. Even though it is clear, you can still see outlines of energy within it. Set the intention that what you do to the lava lamp will be done to the light bodies.

6.) Set the intention, or visualize, that all energy that does not belong to you is being pulled out of your light body and is being placed on the left side of the lava lamp. See a blue flame in the shape of the ball blowing up the cord that was connecting you to the energy that was removed.

7.) Set the intention, or visualize, that all energy that DOES belong to you is being pulled out of the lava lamp and is being place to the right side of the lava lamp. See another blue flame ball blowing up the cord between the lava lamp and YOUR energy that was removed from it.

8.) Connect the energy that is *not* yours to the golden light from Source and the pink light from the Earth. Set the intention that it is being sent back to its original place. Visualize the lava lamp pulling in and absorbing the energy, and pushing it towards the light bodies it belongs to.

9.) Connect *your* energy to the gold and pink light. Also see a white ball of light coming from Source, filling up your energy, and restoring every single cell. See your energy coming into your light body/the hologram of your light body and filling it out completely.

10.) See a blue flame ball coming from Source and blowing up the cord connecting your light body and physical body to the lava lamp. See a 2nd blue flame ball coming from Source and blowing up the *portal* connecting you to the lava lamp and the light bodies. Even after we cut a cord, we need to close the portal that allowed it to be attached. When you see the blue flame ball blowing up the portal, see the blue flame blasting, then condensing into a thin beam of light, then disappearing.

If you are doing this energy work on someone else or your spirit baby, change the perspective of how you are visualizing it. Instead of seeing their light body in front of you, you'd visualize from a bird's eye view perspective within the white dome. Make sure to put on your (and the other's) energetic shield after.

dome. Make sure to put on your (and the other's) energetic shield after. You can also use this cord cutting practice for your embryos if you are on the path of IVF.

You can set the intention to only have your spirit babies corded into your embryos.

When doing the cord cutting practice on an embryo, you will also visualize its light body. Instead of it being in the form of a human like we may picture when doing it on ourselves, it will be a replica of the embryo's current physical state.

If you are working with multiple embryos, see all of the light bodies being corded into one big hologram of them, just like how we do with the light bodies and the lava lamp from those we are cutting cords from.

Just like with surrogacy and sperm donation, a spirit baby may be corded into only 1 parent that allows the energetic freedom to choose how conception occurs. The same applies to IUI.

Just like with IVF, IUI creates a portal for the spirit baby. However, the success of IUI can be influenced by the strength of the spirit baby's cord connection to both parents who intend to raise them. For women who are using IUI (along with a sperm donor, and without a partner who intends to be a parent,) the spirit baby only needs to be corded into her. For couples who are together, whether heterosexual or same sex, or using a sperm donor or not, should focus on ensuring the spirit baby establishes a cord connection with *both* intended parents. Below is a practice you can do with your partner to cord your spirit baby into both of you! If you are planning to conceive naturally, you can use this practice as well!

1.) Sitting facing your partner, visualize yourself being connected to the golden light from Source and the pink light from the Earth. Then visualize the same for your partner!

2.) Put on your energetic shield (Refer back to Chapter 2 for these steps)

3.) Visualize the entire room you are in being filled with a royal purple light

4.) Say in your mind or out loud 3 times, with your partner, "We set the intention to call in our spirit baby." Also set the intention that your spirit babies energy will hover above the empty space between you and your partner.

5.) Visualize a golden and white light from Source filling up your spirit baby's energy, then separating into 2 beams of light radiating over you and your partner. Feel your body absorbing this light.

6.) At the same time, you and your partner visualize a green cord coming from your heart chakras, meeting at chest level in between the both of you, then extending as one beam up to your spirit baby.

7.) See your spirit baby recycle the green light into 2 beams, one towards you and one towards your partner. You each absorb the green beam of light through the top of your head, streaming down into your heart, and branching out like vines down throughout your entire body.

8.) Visualize a glittery white ball of light from Source coming down from the sky and encompassing you, your partner, and your spirit baby

And that's all there is to it!

When you feel the urge to strengthen the cord between you and your spirit baby, you can set the intention for your spirit baby to feel the green heart cord. Or, you can do this practice as many times as you feel called to!

Step Parents, Foster Parents, and Choosing Alternative Parental Figures

Souls who have foster parents began unconsciously attracting them after birth. When planning out a lifetime, there are different levels of soul agreements that are made. Some agreements are looser, while other soul agreements are significant (such as two souls deciding they will have children with one another, and a spirit baby is corded into both of them.) When the soul of a child who has already been born begins unconsciously seeking parental figures, and people who desire to become foster parents begin putting plans into motion, they begin to attract one another into each other's lives.

These soul agreements tend to start off "looser", and if the soul and the foster parents bond on a deep level their spiritual connection grows stronger. It is a connection that is nurtured over time.

The love and care provided by foster parents fulfill deep soul desires, shaping the child's development and emotional growth, while offering the foster parents a chance to fulfill their own spiritual missions.

For children who become exchange students, or spend significant periods of time with other parental figures, the spirit baby connection can still appear in the energy of those other than the biological parents. Whether they are raised in different cultural contexts, spend extended time away from their biological parents, or are guided by mentors and caregivers, these souls can still appear as spirit babies in the energy of those who care for them. The spiritual bonds transcend physical proximity and family structure, revealing that a spirit baby's attachment to parental figures is not limited to one traditional relationship. The essence of the child will show up in the energy of those who have committed to playing a parental role in their life, even temporarily.

Like with foster parenting, in the case of an exchange student, mentor, or temporary caregiver, a loose soul agreement is established and will physically manifest if the child's soul, and the other person or people's souls, desire to make it a reality based on their current circumstances.

Step-parenting is also a powerful dynamic that can arise from soul agreements. Each of us has soul contracts with others based on the path of our lives, and these agreements often involve multiple romantic relationships or potential family dynamics. While we may have more than one romantic soul agreement, only those aligned with the timing, growth, and lessons of each person will materialize in the physical world. For a spirit baby, these agreements can extend beyond the birth parents, allowing them to form bonds with step-parents or other significant figures as the family dynamic evolves. Step-parents, therefore, are not just circumstantial figures but are often meant to play vital roles in the child's spiritual journey.

Spirit babies are remarkably aware of the potential connections that their parents may have with future partners. Even before the child arrives on Earth, they can sense and begin forming bonds with individuals who may later become romantically involved with their parent. These spirit babies possess a deep knowing that their journey will involve not just one, but potentially several caregivers, who will play a role in their growth and development. The spirit baby can communicate energetically with potential step-parents, preparing them for the shared experience of parenting and helping create a harmonious environment for their arrival. In these instances, the soul agreements extend beyond just the biological parent-child relationship and include other partners who will be pivotal in the child's life.

It is said it takes a village to raise a child, and it also takes a a village to put plans in place to cover every possibility, outcome, and path during this physical lifetime before being born.

In essence, the connection between spirit babies and their caregivers is fluid, extending across various family dynamics. Whether a child is raised by foster parents, step-parents, or other significant figures, these relationships are not coincidences but are part of the intricate design of soul agreements. These bonds form well before physical birth and continue to evolve as the child grows, embracing new parental figures along the way. By understanding the spiritual roots of these relationships, we can appreciate the deeper soul connections that shape the experiences of both the child and the caregiver.

Part 3

Short Lessons
and
Transmissions

Chapter 17: Nice and Cozy!

Ironically, as a medium I choose not to see other beings with my physical eye. Sometimes you need to draw the line when your non-physical senses are turned on and activated every day! However, when looking into students' and clients' energies, I will see with my third eye the auras of spirit babies within their energy.

Spirit babies LOVE to make themselves home by dwelling by one or more parts of their parent's body.

Where they show up on the body is a reflection of where they are currently trying to support their parent based on the energetic root of that part of the body. Our body is a messenger for what is happening in and around us on an energetic and unconscious level, so the spirit baby will attach to the parts of our body that need healing or that they feel comfortable around!

Read through this quick breakdown of the meaning behind different parts of the body that spirit babies will most commonly pop up in, and see if they relate to where you feel your spirit baby around your body!

Top of the Head: Encouraging the parent's thoughts and wisdom, or providing calming energy from the parent's racing thoughts

Third Eye: Helping the parent activate their intuition, and see new perspectives

Shoulders: Providing support when a lot is going on, or helping to release burdens

Heart: Helping the parent to be able to give and receive love without hesitation, worry, or anxiety

Forearms and Hands: Encouraging the parent to step into their full strength and take charge over how things go in their life

Solar Plexus: Providing confidence and authority in the parent's behavior

Womb: This is definitely a spirit baby favorite! Since the womb will be the home for their physical body to develop, they love to hang out in and around the womb energetically. The womb represents sensuality, creativity, femininity, and manifestation

Chapter 18: Transcending the Physical: Part 1, For Moms to Be

In this chapter, we're going to approach it with a free flowing intention on what the spirit baby realm wants to share.

The first image coming through is one that is full of innocence and joy! At first, a pink cosmo flower opens up its petals and a fairy-like creature emerges from the center of the flower with open arms. She slides down one of the petals and is seen hopping amusingly from one flower to another. She is then shown with wings as she begins to delicately fly upwards until sparkles fluttering from her wings are magnetized towards the energy of the spirit baby we will be connecting with today.
I am now asking the spirit baby who has joined us today to introduce themselves and a message for us to receive.

"Hello! My name is Mira. It is so good to meet with you today!" She spins around and smiles ear to ear to express her excitement. She continues, "You may have seen a little fairy guide you to me today. She is one of my spirit guides and can shape shift into any Earthly creature. She will be one of the guides assisting me to Earth, and she loves to spend time there and imprint the energy from her experiences into my aura so I can experience the feelings of being on Earth before I even get there! I'm sensing that there are some receiving this message who might be feeling like the journey to conceiving is hard. And sometimes, it certainly does feel that way! However it is important to know that you are a fairy. Stick with me here!

You are in a human body. You are having a human experience. But the energy of conception can be that of delight. It can be as freeing as the experience of hopping from petal to petal. Except, instead of hopping from petal to petal, you are transitioning from one state of being to another. This is nothing to fear.

In fact, I'd encourage you to see fear as expansion, or like the feeling of getting a massage when something that has been tight in your body for so long is finally breaking free. We spirit babies are here to help you move through this. Do you think nine months of pregnancy is random? Nope! Nine is a potent number that we use here in the spirit baby realm. One of the highest frequencies is that of 900 hertz, which is a frequency that occurs with peace and harmony. This is also the frequency that angels vibrate in! So, in your nine months of pregnancy, you can use this time to allow yourself to calibrate to the frequency of expanding not only your family but yourself too!

Stagnancy is a myth. You are constantly growing and evolving. When it seems like things are stuck, or like your path to welcoming in your spirit baby isn't happening, know that we are always here for you. It is not just our job to join your family in the physical, but to be a guiding light for you in every area of life. Need a little more time? We understand. Feeling angry and need to let it out? We get it! Feeling like you need to take a break from calling us in? It's no problem!

Motherhood is more than diapers and staying up in the middle of the night. It's more than doctor's appointments and everyone around you asking when you're due. It's an initiation into something that will leave an imprint on your soul for millennials to come. The connections you are making with your spirit baby will fill your soul with love and fulfillment that will last beyond your physical body and beyond your current physical lifetime. No matter what you are going through in the physical, the energy always stays. You will always have a soul. Your spirit baby, even once you bring them into this world, will have a soul. Know that the foundation for your relationship with your spirit baby, your pregnancy, and motherhood have already been set. It has already been decided. Know that by you receiving this message, there is a spirit baby with you. No matter what your relationship looks like with them now, they are always there to guide you into love, safety, peace, and harmony. Allow yourself to listen. Allow yourself to feel. It is okay to surrender. It is okay to trust the process, even if you are unsure how the process will unfold. Be present. By present, I mean allowing the unfolding of who you are becoming. You deserve to be the sexy mama, the spiritual mama, the colorful mama, the creative mama, or whatever resonates with you. Motherhood will plunge you into your gifts. These gifts might be just for yourself. It might be for your family. It might be for the world. Or all three! They already exist within you, and your spirit baby is the biggest cheerleader in you opening up to your authenticity, like the threshold crossed just before you erupt into boisterous laughter! You got this mama! We love you."

Chapter 19: Transcending the Physical: Part 2, For Dads to Be

I am shown in my third eye a group of male souls huddling close together, solely focusing on their almost ceremony-like gathering. Their golden auras fade up and down like a candle burning. I observe their closeness, and the comfort they have in the proximity of one another. Their gathering exudes a holy essence that I do not want to disturb. The way they receive each other's closeness and the way they focus on their intention is hypnotic. Like we've learned throughout this book, spirit babies operate from a baseline of love and compassion. They have a calling to heal, to encourage, and to celebrate.

These spirit babies are aware of my presence, yet wish to remain in silence.

I ask to feel their compassion and love going into this chapter. I ask for them to support me in finding the words that will speak to the men who will read this chapter. They welcome my request, and remain focused on their gathering.

If you are a woman reading this, now is the time to get cozy on the couch with your partner, or let them know that there is an excerpt you'd love for them to read. This chapter is for the men who believe it is part of their purpose to have children and a family, and to give their love and devotion to you and the children who will see him as a leader and protector of the family. Fathers are underestimated.
.

Sometimes the seas get turbulent. The rough push of the wave makes you want to turn around, to give up, or to give space until the storm passes over. But your dear partner and children long to be safe in the cabin where they know all things of now will pass. They may shiver in anxiety. Your partner may grip the wheel and look upon the horizon, trying to feel her way to safety. Yet you place a hand on her shoulder, slowly guiding her away, and you wrap your arms around your children where their tears come to a pause and their limbs become like jello because they are safe in your arms. Your presence is the remedy, the magic, the energy to bring peace and order to all.

Fathers are the initiator of the spirit baby's journey.

If you and your partner have felt the longing, the yearning, and the desire to bring your children Earthside, do not fear the journey.

You may wonder,
"What if I screw up?"
"What if I can't provide for my family?"
"What if I'm not good enough?"
"What if it's just not meant to be?"

But what if it IS?
Your spirit baby has chosen you, and trusts your part in their path to Earth.

A spirit baby will amplify a woman's intuition, her deepest desires, and the emotions that want to burst through her body to be seen and heard.

A spirit baby will reflect to a man all of the potential that he is and will continue to be. Before you begin thinking about the weight you may already feel like you have on your shoulders, or begin to entertain the trials and tribulations that may arise in the future, notice your body's reaction.

Do you want to retract?
Do you want to step away?
Are your shoulders and palms braced as if you are about to enter in your battle?

If you knew your spirit baby trusted you, no matter your decision, how would move through the world?

This is a question that your spirit baby is encouraging you to embody Every. Single. Day. It is not about proving your worth. It is not about becoming something perfect, and looking for one problem after another to fix because the cycle never feels complete.

Imagine your potential to be a cocktail of ingredients that, while may seem opposites on their own, blended together spark a feeling of delight.

Your potential is an embodiment of all of who you are, all of who present yourself to be in the world, and all of what you desire to provide your family and the world.

All the while, your spirit baby is cheering on, "Go Daddy go!"

My attention is brought back to the group of souls from the beginning of this chapter, and they stand in a line, holding hands and each taking on the face of an older man.

The soul to the far right shares, "We have each walked this path before. Many times. Not just a few children in one lifetime, but dozens of children throughout multiple lifetimes. We've made mistakes. We've allowed ourselves to be distracted, and bribed, and told what we were and weren't doing good enough. The only ruler of your life is you. And being a father means that you are the guardian to your own kingdom where *you* decide your own reality and that of your family's.

Who are you without the noise? Because trust me, there will be a lot of it; not just the pitter patter of your children's feet running across the floor, or the sound of your partner baking chocolate chip cookies, but the seeds of suggestions from others.

'Why don't you do this? Why don't you do that? You should think about this. You should think about that. Come do this for me.'

It is up to you to know how this effects your kingdom.
Knowing isn't always the logical solution.
Sometimes it is a feeling in your gut.
It is the tugging in your chest guiding you to where you need to go.
Trust yourself, and your kingdom will trust you. They want to give you all of the love, care, and nourishment in the world. Do not think that you are not capable. Your potential is not a burden, but the key to your freedom. Your spirit

baby knows and sees this. They will walk with you through anything. They can't wait until they day where they can feel you tossing them up in the air and knowing you'll be there to catch them. They know you'll be there for every tear, every heartbreak, and that you'll be the loudest in the room to celebrate them. You, father, are irreplaceable."

Chapter 20: There's a Bond to Be Built

(Channeled from one of my spirit babies)

At the time of writing this chapter, I've been blessed with a week that has been full of my spirit baby's presence. It was almost comical to see how many times she showed up through a lady bug, which is one of the main symbols of communication we have together!

It started when on a Sunday night, I noticed a lady bug on the window, but it flew away too quickly and I didn't see it again.

Two days later, I walked into the bedroom then turned around to see a lady bug had flown into the room and it proceeded to land on my back. I took the lady bug outside.

Then a couple of days after that, I bought 2 new glass cutting boards with butterflies on it and didn't realize that it also had ladybugs on it.

To a stranger it might seem like it is all coincidence, but when you build a bond with your spirit baby you begin to easily notice when they are communicating with you.

Something that is even more miraculous is when you catch yourself thinking of your spirit baby, and they send you a sign immediately after. (This happens to me ALL of the time!)

Along the journey of desiring to become a parent, it is easy to forget that outside of the desire and the calling is a soul who has already decided that they want to come. The only thing is, they need (and want) your trust in knowing that they will come when it feels aligned for them.

Just like any relationship, spirit babies desire to be trusted, heard, and they also want you to be able to trust yourself.

I've called in my spirit baby to share insight on building a bond with your spirit baby.

"We agreed on this before birth. We agreed to meet again in this life." *My spirit baby is referring to herself and I.*

"All spirit babies will choose their parents at different times, whether it is before the parents are even born, or 6 months before they want to be conceived, but there is never a spirit baby who hasn't made the conscious decision to be yours.

Think of how amazing and honorable that is. They. Chose. YOU! One day, you will hear their laugh. Their smile will light up a room. And you will wonder if your heart will be able to hold even more love than it already does. What if I told you it is possible to feel that with your spirit baby right now?

Time moves much slower on Earth than it does for a spirit baby. What may be 1 month to you may only be a minute for a spirit baby. Your access to your speed of time is a gift. You have the opportunity to to milk the minutes of the day and spend them with a soul who wants to know you; ALL of you!

A spirit baby does not judge (unless in good humor!) A spirit baby will not criticize you and tell you that you are doing something wrong. Your spirit baby will be the loving teacher you didn't know you needed, and it is 100% safe to explore that dynamic!

Just because you are choosing to become a parent doesn't mean you cannot be held, supported, and guided.

It is your spirit baby's pleasure to hold you and guide you.

There will never be another time like this;
Where your spirit baby can take on the form of an animal, a number, or even a *feeling* within your body just to be with you and let you know that they are with you.

In your moments of sadness, pain, and confusion, your spirit baby is saying 'Ah, but wait until you see my plan.'

Source, too, is agreeing with your spirit baby and is saying, 'The best is yet to come.'

The bond between you and your spirit baby is like no other.

There's a practice I will share with you so you can feel a closer bond to your spirit baby, and hope along your journey."

Be sure to do the energetic practice from Chapter 2 before closing your eyes, calling in your spirit baby, and doing this practice.

"Visualize that you are in an art gallery. Paintings are lined up side by side along a golden wall. The similarity between each painting is that it is of a family. There are paintings of the family growing, the family playing, and the family being present with one another.

Notice the colors, the expressions, and the scenes of each painting. Keep walking further into the gallery until you notice that there are no more paintings to see.

In your mind's eye, turn around and realize that each painting was a montage of *your* life.

Now, start to walk back the same way you came, but now knowing that the beauty of your life is what is on display.

Where are you in the paintings?
What did it take for you to get there?
What kind of life did you provide for your children?

There's nothing a spirit baby loves more than to feel that their parent(s) feel open and *free.*

Once you get back to where you started, you notice the artist of the paintings is standing there.

Except the artist is your spirit baby.

Your spirit baby has laid out for you in color, beauty, and boldness the kind of life that you both want to have together.

Allow yourself a few moments to connect with your spirit

baby. If you have a question for your spirit baby, you can ask them in your mind or out loud to draw you a painting depicting the answer to your question."

The beautiful thing about this practice that my spirit baby is sharing is that it'll also help you to uncover any unconscious thoughts, feelings, or concerns that you have around your current situation and the future. Our unconscious mind loves to use symbolism to communicate with us, and our intuition does the same.

Once you feel like you've received a response, or spent the amount of time with your spirit baby that you wanted, you can watch the scene fade away and re-do the energetic protection practice from Chapter 2 to seal off your aura and come back into your body.

My spirit baby continues, "It doesn't matter how long you build the bond, as long as the bond is built. Just as you would with a friend, or marriage partner, you would take the time to get to know them, their personality, and what they want out of life. Your spirit baby is no different, except, they are not verbally speaking to you in a human body. Instead of asking your spirit baby, 'Where are you?' or 'Why are you taking long to come?' ask them:

'What makes you feel supported?'
'What role are we meant to play in each other's lives?'
'How can I align with the highest-frequency version of myself so you can come in with ease?'
'How can I show you my love for you?'

With these questions, you get to know your spirit baby and form a bond that *literally* transcends lifetimes."

I am taking a deep breath here because my spirit baby always speaks in the most philosophical ways! The wisdom of spirit babies is utterly magical and I cannot imagine this world without receiving the love they have to share.

I am now taking a few moments to thank my spirit baby, and to feel into my heart and womb.

No matter where you are, or what you are doing, you can call upon your spirit baby at any time.

Chapter 21: Guided by Your Inner Compass - Trusting Your Intuition

(Channeled from one of my spirit babies)

"You see, your inner compass is like the north star shining the light to lead you in finding your way. It's the part of you that knows. It's the part of you that yearns and desires for better and brighter things to come into your life. But your inner compass, or your intuition, is also the part of you that is the biggest reflection. It'll show you your fears. It'll show you your doubts. And you will have moments where your intuition's voice is dimmed because you feel like there is no other possibility or way out. When you are feeling unclear, come back to this; 'Uncertainty is safe. I already have the tools I need to handle any solution that comes my way. I know that the universe is here to support me. My intuition is a piece of the universe that I get to carry inside of me. I know that I am guided. I know that I am supported. These feelings of fear or doubt do not mean that they are actually a threat. These feelings actually allow me to practice the beautiful art of surrender that will bring me back to my inner voice.' Know that no matter what is hindering you from hearing your intuition right now, coming back to your heart will lead the way. Your heart is a gateway to your inner compass/intuition. Let what you feel in your heart radiate throughout your body.

This exquisite dance of life was perfectly designed. Know that with your intuition, which was with you since before you were born, was meant to be the sanctuary that you seek.

The more you can trust, the more you can surrender, and the deeper you can experience the fullness of life, the clearer your intuition will become. When you look up into the night sky and see the brightest star shining, be reminded of how this star has guided many people across open seas to new destinations with no clue of what would come. Your feelings may show up like those open seas. The possibilities may feel like those new destinations. But just like that bright star in the sky, your intuition is permanent and will guide you and future generations for lifetimes to come."

Chapter 22: The Illusion of Time

(Channeled from one of my spirit babies)

"Time on the clock is not the same as the time in the cosmos. Time, in essence, is a cycle of beginning and completion. It's the rise and fall of frequencies, and the transmutation of energies from one form to another. You know on Earth when it is October, when it's noon, and when it's the start of a new year. The telling of time marks a new stage of a cycle. Where spirit babies exist, we don't have 24 hour days. We don't have months and years. We do, however, have a sense of feeling change. When you receive a timeframe from a spirit baby, they are using what you know to measure time, as a way of communicating with you. It's a way for you to understand what they see for you (and your spirit baby is always seeing your highest potentials, purpose, and joys!) Truly, time to a spirit baby, or any soul, is felt when multiple frequencies align that cause a change to be underway. When a soul feels this change, that may be their time to jump into a physical body, a time to make their spiritual presence known, or a time to be of service alongside other souls. Imagine two stars colliding, and the impact that they make. Or an earthquake that can be felt even miles away from the initial point of collision. The impact, or the result of the change, is what is felt by a soul. This is the kind of time a soul perceives.

When a soul is aware of this time, their own frequency is impacted by the vibrations of the changes; a domino effect if you will!

It acts as an initiation for a soul to take an action that will create a different experience within their own existence. While time can feel frustrating when you are trying to conceive, know that your core method of telling time is the same as your spirit baby. By observing time from the lens of feeling, openness, and expansion, you have the ability to begin creating the ripple effect that invites your baby into your womb."

Chapter 23: Knowing my Name

Have you ever wondered if there was once a time where we didn't have names? Or have you wondered if there was a time where we didn't a variety of names like we do today, where each one is unique and has meaning? Do you think it may be possible that there are vibrations underneath the names we have and choose that enhance our aura? I once read a book where the author shared an activity that they learned on interpreting our soul purpose and what we are meant to do in this life. It involved looking up the meaning behind each name in your full name, and that statement or combination of words showing you your soul's qualities and purpose. Choosing a name for your baby, or understanding your own, can be an enlightening discovery. Follow along as we channel from the spirit baby realm the importance of names, and how you can choose a name for your baby that feels like the perfect fit.

In my mind's eye, I have been immediately transported to a garden where the breeze is warm and slightly tickles the skin. The weeds and flowers sway, and the sky is a deep blue. I feel as if I am crouching in the grass, tucked away from the world, watching a peaceful yet phenomenon happening. There are balls of light floating mid-air. They are smoothly bouncing up and down like bubbles that never pop. A spirit baby appears and begins juggling and playing with the balls of light. I introduce myself to the spirit baby. The spirit baby introduce's herself with the name Yani.
Of course. because of the nature of this chapter's topic, I am

compelled to look up the name on Google. The name means "calm" and "peaceful." Reading that has sent a shiver of awe and delight into my heart. The spirit baby joining us has shown this scene in particular to represent her own name. What a fine job she did!

I share my thoughts with Yani on how I would like for her to share the importance of names, and how expecting parents can choose the 'right' name for their baby. She is now beginning to explain. Let's receive her guidance:

"Hello beautiful! Thank you for joining me in this sanctuary. It is amazing for you to be here! My aura and personality is very big, so I love to use the images like the one I sent you to introduce myself. I also know how overwhelming it can be sometimes to connect with other realms, and so when I appear I make it important to present myself with calmness and serenity."

I share with her that I looked up her name and tbat it means "calm" and "peaceful."

She continues,
"Yes, I knew that!" she giggles, "But my name didn't come first. The feeling came first. The vibration came first. The humming sounds from my soul's creation came first. Physical names are a way that humans get to play with sound. There are sounds that exist that humans are unable to hear. However, each sound audible to the human ear has more underneath tones of it that activates many

vibrations within the cosmos. When each soul is created, a unique tone can be felt by other souls. This tone is not something that can be thought of or interpreted by the human mind. However, it can be felt through the heart or the use of intuition. Think of it like this; there are dog whistles that while are very very hard to hear with a human ear, can be heard loudly by the dog's ear.

When it comes to names, you have the chance to piece together multiple sounds and tones to evoke a feeling within you. When you say my name, you probably feel a sense of lightness and playful beauty. When you say your name, you may notice feelings that come up around your own identity.

The meanings around names, that humans have created, are a result of each culture or society's experiences, surroundings, and feelings within their heart.

Names are not just a way of addressing and differentiating between people. They are a way of connecting to a person's soul self.

When you choose a name for your spirit baby, get to know their presence first. Without a name, what do they feel like in your heart? What signs do they enjoy sending you? What images do they show you when you close your eyes? Take in their essence. Luckily, you have many physical tools as well to discover names that you may not currently know of. As you look through these names, hold your spirit baby's essence close to you. Decide from there what name illuminates their soul self. When I refer to the soul self, I am referring to the culmination of their gifts, previous lifetime experiences, and what they are planning for in this next one. This name will be their identity in this lifetime. That name can activate miracles! It is wonderful alignment when the soul-self of someone, and their physical name, harmonize energetically and make that person radiate in every room they walk into. It's like a puzzle piece that perfectly fits.

If you knew the name that you choose for your spirit baby would represent and amplify all of their experiences and who they desire to be in this lifetime, what would you choose?"

I thank Yani for sharing her advice, and her presence disappears from my minds eye.

Chapter 24: Tackling Fears Around Parenthood

(Channeled from one of my spirit babies)

"You may feel like you are not ready. You may feel like the world around you is crumbling with anxiety and excitement all at the same time. You may feel like you don't know a thing about being a parent and how you could possibly raise another human being based on what you already know.

Knowing that your baby has already chosen you may feel like an extra weight on your shoulders, but let me remind you; you and your baby are made up of the same energy. You both have a soul. You both have a consciousness. You are both going through the human experience yet at different paces.

This little baby will be a reflection of you, and that may feel scary. But let me remind you that you are also guided by something greater. You might not have all of the answers, but Source does. Let them hold your fears, your doubts, and your worries. Know that before your baby is birthed here too, they are willing to take on and hold what you are feeling. They understand the shifts that will be happening in your mind and body as they begin to make their way to Earth. It is a mutual journey that you will both get to experience together.

You might be pondering the finances, how to set up the baby's room, the doctor's appointments, and your health. Know that your spirit baby is pondering things too! Your spirit baby is planning their life purpose, what they will learn in this lifetime, and the relationship that they will have with you. You are not alone in this journey, both physically and spiritually."

My spirit baby then shows an image of the Earth rotating, and light beams begin to pop up in various places until the light blends like a glowing orb. My spirit baby points to this image acknowledging how we are all connected.

They continue, "Understand that your fears do not exist where you are from. When you were a spirit baby, you existed in a place where harmony and high frequencies of love were the normal. Earth is a challenge. It's okay to admit that! All spirit babies who choose to come to Earth are also aware of this, but are excited for all of the things they will experience that do not exist in other realms. Your fear gets to be your teacher. If your fear were a reflection in the mirror, what would they say?

At first they may say, "This isn't going to work out," or, "I don't know if I am fit to do this!" But what if fear were a messenger for what Source or your spirit baby were trying to guide you on? What if your fear was a wise teacher with lifetimes of wisdom and knowledge? What if your fear brought out the greatest parts of you and the most authentic pieces of your soul? Also, I am totally hinting to you to try this practice for real in a mirror!

Everyone's journey to parenthood looks different, as everyone's soul agrees upon different conditions and relationships with one another. You get to focus on YOUR relationship with your spirit baby. The energetic and spiritual connection you will have with your spirit baby will be unlike anyone else's. It is unique to you. Hold that in your heart. Allow that love to guide you along your journey.

When you are led by your heart, and by the energies that brought you here that will now be bringing. your spirit baby to you, you are able to surrender to clarity. You can release the how. You can find joy in the void before your spirit baby arrives. And when they do, you will be free."

Part 4:
Embodying Agape

Who is love to you?
Not what, WHO?

If love physically showed up on your door step today, what would they look like to you? Maybe they'd be radiating with the brightest smile, or maybe they'd look worn down, tired, and at their wits' end. The good news is, love isn't limited to one body. Love isn't limited to one path. Love is infinite, and commands our awareness in every day life. When we are worried about the never-ending to do lists, or the fears we have in our mind, love is grasping for my attention.

Love is saying, "Look at me! I am here in the beauty of the cherry blossom tree in your back yard!"
"Look at me! The banana you are about to eat is full of nutrients that will nurture your body.
"Look at me! I am in the clean air your breathe each day."

Love desires to be seen, heard, and felt on a daily basis. We have romantic love, familial love, love for our friends, and then we have agape. (Pronounced a-gah-peh.) Agape is the love that is unconditional, unrestricted by the fleeting tide of our emotions, and is the highest form of love that requires our daily commitment to something higher and greater.

Agape simply exists.
Agape is always present, and makes itself known.
Agape does not seek to be chosen, but in our choosing of it we choose ourselves, our soul, and our faith in the love and wisdom that exists beyond our physical body. All spirit

babies, no matter their purpose, parents, or life of choosing, say "yes" to the spiritual path of returning to knowing, and deciding, to commit to a love greater than our emotions; a love that creates every soul and every being.

Agape created you, and it created your spirit babies. Where agape is claimed, life is created, multiplied, and given a freedom that can only be given by an essence that knows love is not an energy to be controlled, but a way of being that is chosen. When you place your hand on your womb, and your mind flashes memories of the spirit babies you have birthed, or that departed early, or that have yet to come, this is when Agape is ready to be chosen the most; when we find the liberation in,

"I feel like my body is broken, but it was designed by love. And love will create the family I desire."

"I feel like giving up, but love brought me here with the strength of a million suns."

"I am scared, but the love that created my child gave them the freedom to choose ME. They trust me, and I can trust me too."

Your soul was designed by love, by *Agape*.

Your spirit baby, aware of their own creation and yours, embodies Agape and sends it to you every single day. Even though in definition we say Agape is a higher love, it is does not require you to look up at the sky, and to wonder if this higher love is somewhere far far above your own physical body. We can find solace when we look up at the stars and feel the mystical gleam of the moon. We can find peace when we look up to pray, and come back to the grounded existence of our own physical body.

Higher love, however, is expanded consciousness, deeper capacities, and openness to receive the love and life that is all around you. Your spirit baby, while could quite literally be existing in a realm physically higher, makes their presence known in the breeze that brushes your shoulders, the tingling in your heart, and the laughter in your dreams.

Place your palms out in front of you.
Now lift them up, and bring them together.

Feel the closeness, and the space of your palms, coexisting at once.

Invisible to our physical eye, millions of particles are moving, vibrating, combusting, and existing. Think of how many times these particles, so perfectly existing together, multiplied to create YOU.

Your spirit baby's pure existence is an embodiment of Agape. And the physical manifestation of your spirit baby's soul is another product of love expanding over and over and over again.

No matter the journey, the destination is inevitable. Love always finds a way. The love for your spirit baby, and your spirit baby's love in return, is the wish on the star that brings your baby into your arms.

Thank You

For reading "The Spirit Baby Diaries"

The final page of the book is a dedicated space to writing a love letter to your spirit baby, or your babies already Earthside that you'd like to have as a keepsake for them.

With love,

Katie Ubele

Scan the QR code

To leave a review on Amazon, follow Katie on socials, and explore all spirit baby resources:

to my baby, with love

www.ingramcontent.com/pod-product-compliance
Lightning Source LLC
Chambersburg PA
CBHW071513120626
46550CB00006B/2209